PENNSBURY POTTERY

Lucile Henzke

Schiffer Publishing Ltd

1469 Morstein Road, West Chester, Pennsylvania 19380

Pennsbury group depicting various shapes and designs. 13½" Charger at back. "Slaying the Dragon". Second row: 6¼" "Amish Pitcher", ash tray "Outen the Light", tray "Horses", and #114 "Wood Duck" 10". Front row: 2½" pitcher "Amish Boy", "Amish" salt and pepper figurals (two sizes), Pennsbury "Display" sign, and "Rooster" candle holder.

Library of Congress Catalog Number: 89-64083.

Printed in the United States of America.
ISBN: 0-88740-229-1

Published by Schiffer Publishing, Ltd.
1469 Morstein Road
West Chester, Pennsylania 19380
Please write for a free catalog
This book may be purchased from the publisher.
Please include $2.00 postage.
Try your bookstore first.

Title page photo:
Pottery display sign 5" x 4½". Note bird was made on the same mold as the "Slick-Chick".

Contents

8¼'' Toleware Cookie Jar.

Acknowledgments

To Esther O. Keller, we wish to convey our deepest gratitude and many thanks. Without her assistance and diligent research this chapter, on the history of American pottery, would never have been as thorough.

The author also wishes to express her sincere thanks to former personnel of the Pennsbury, Glen View and Pennington Potteries for sharing their personal memories and knowledge concerning the subjects in this book. Also, to the many friends who searched for rarities and shared their collections and information. Without their vast interest, this treatise would never have been as complete. To the following, our profound gratitude is owed.

Helen F. Brown, Betty and Floyd Carson, Susan Cox, Edith Guilfoy, Evelyn Guilfoy, Shirley Graff, Barbara and Norman Haas, Peter K. Hexter, Mary Jane Hillegass, Louis (Lou) Hohn, Phyllis Larson, Levittown Courier Times, Alma Roberts, Kathryne Strine, B.A. Wellman, and the Pennsylvania Government Agencies-who were always co-operative. Recognition must also be given to Mary and Frank Smith for the wealth of information contributed.

A special acknowledgment is given to a dear friend, Joyce Smalley, who always unselfishly shared her vast collection and information. Also, a special thanks to Ozella and D.L. Hill for first introducing us to the Pennsbury creations and to Jerry Henzke for the photography.

3 "Amish" Coffee Mugs. Illustrating color variations.

Respectfully Dedicated
To Esther O. Keller.

6½'' Eagle Figural #P215

12'' high ''Hex'' Lamp. Collection of Joyce Smalley.

Foreword

The primary subject of this book, is Pennsbury Pottery. However, three other Potteries are listed due to a connection with Pennsbury, namely: Glen View, Pennington and Lewis Brothers.

When Pennsbury closed, in 1970, Glen View continued to market Pennsbury 1970 "Angel" Christmas plates, using the original markings on the back. Later, when Pennington took over Glen View, they also continued to market the "Angel" plate. Both Potteries produced other items, using the recognized Pennsbury color. Most of these items were plates with different designs, however, all items were marked with the company name that produced them. Evidently, the Pennsbury color was very popular.

A 1970 Stumar Christmas Plate, "Angel". First edition, marked Pennsbury.

Lewis Brothers Pottery was started in 1946, by Alton and Sanford Lewis. Their connection with Pennsbury differs from the other two Potteries. At the demise of Pennsbury, Lewis Brothers purchased about fifty of the lesser molds. Though the name Pennsbury was to be removed from these molds, some pieces escaped this removal and, consequently, some articles were sold to customers with the Pennsbury name showing. An agreement was reached after Mr. Ernst Below threatened litigation, and no action was taken. Not removing the name Pennsbury was probably an honest mistake. Molds were changed, somewhat, as to design, sayings and shapes. No Harvest or Rooster patterns, plaques, birds or any unusual molds, such as the highly decorated pieces, were included in the purchase.

When Lewis Brothers first started their business, they probably created articles of stoneware and some porcelain pieces. When they purchased the Pennsbury molds, they began producing hand decorated pottery pieces. Incidently, Lewis Brothers did produce a near likeness of the Pennsbury Hen and Rooster, even though the mold was also changed to some extent. Enthusiastic Pennsbury collectors can definitely differentiate between the original and the so called look-a-likes.

Further discussion of the Glen View, Pennington and Lewis Brothers potteries appears at the end of the Pennsbury story.

9½" Commemorative Pie Pan. Shoo-Fly-Pie. Dutch Haven.

Pennsbury Pottery History

The Pennsbury Pottery, one of the last creators of fine and unusual hand decorated art wares in America, was located three miles west of Morrisville, Pennsylvania. This area is in historical Bucks County, which is up river from Pennsbury Manor, home of William Penn, founder of Pennsylvania.

It is recorded at the Bucks County Courthouse, Recorder of Deeds Office, that on May 29, 1950, Henry and Lee Below (pronounced like Bell-o) purchased 2.207 acres of land in Falls Township; Deed Book 946-209. The Pennsbury Pottery was erected on this acreage and opened for business later in the year. The Pottery adopted the name "Pennsbury" due to the proximity of Pennsbury Manor. Several years prior to this opening; on May 20, 1939, Henry and Lee Below purchased thirty plus acres of land in Falls Township, Bucks County; Deed Book 678-322, presumably for a farm. On December 27, 1949, they disposed of this same acreage, Deed Book 928-355. The proceeds from this sale enabled them to start the pottery business, a dream of theirs for a long time.

The new enterprise soon began to prosper, owing to the experience and expertise of the Below family. Optimism and determination also contributed immensely to a successful business that remained vigorous for several years. Henry was an expert in ceramic engineering and mold making, having worked several years, in that capacity, for the Stangl Pottery in Trenton, New Jersey. Lee Below was also a talented artist, designer and modeler, who had previously worked for Stangl as well. She designed the ever popular "Rooster" patterns, the "Folkart" and other intriguing designs that depict scenes and quotations indigenous to the folklore of the vicinity.

5" "Red Rooster" beverage mug. Collection Joyce Smalley.

"Red Rooster" 10" plate.

An 8" "Courting Buggy" Plate, signed "S" Sue Below.

A 6" "Harvest" Tile, signed LB.

At the time Henry and Lee embarked upon their new project, they had been married for nineteen years and were the parents of three children; Sue, nineteen; Ernst H. seventeen; and Greta, eleven years of age. Later, Ernst succeeded his father as general manager of the company. Sue spent some time at the Pottery, in the decorating department. She is known to have decorated several pieces, including some of the birds. Evelyn Guilfoy, an employee, related: "Sue was especially good at working on the larger birds." Work done by Sue, are generally signed with a single "S".

It is recorded in Book 94, page 239, at the Buck County, Pennsylvania Courthouse, that Henry and Lee Below were married on July 11, 1931, by a Justice of the Peace. This information, concerning the marriage, is revealed on the application as follows:

Wedding date—July 11, 1931
Henry Below—Chemist. Born in Bavaria, Germany.
Residence—Feasterville, Pennsylvania. Age 27
Father—Max Below. Dentist. Landshut, Germany.
Mother—Freda Zaltach Below. Landshut, Germany.
Lee Ehrlich—Modeler, Designer. Born in Breman, Germany.
Residence—Feasterville, Pennsylvania. Age 25
Father—Gustave Ehrlich. Breman, Germany.
Mother—Freda Menlenson Ehrlich. Breman, Germany.

Henry's father wanted his son to become a dentist instead of going into the pottery business.

Evidently, they were a loving family, since many of the articles they designed are decorated with families, lovers, hearts and other symbols of happiness, such as birds. It was definitely a sad day when Henry Below suddenly passed away, on December 21, 1959. It has been said "He was a hard worker, putting in many hours." His death was an unexpected shock to everyone, since he had been at work the previous day and had not been ill. He was 55 years old at the time. His obituary appeared in the Levittown Courier Times. Mr. Below was listed as founder of the Pennsbury Pottery and had died at his home, next to the Pottery. Prior to starting his own business, in 1950, he was plant manager at the Stangl Pottery in Trenton, New Jersey. The paper also revealed that Henry Below was a member of the New Jersey Ceramic Association and past president of the Morrisville Rotary Club. He was also member of the Philadelphia Chapter of Schlaraffia America. In addition to his wife and mother, Mr. Below was survived by a son; Ernst H. of Morrisville, two daughters; Mrs. Samuel Heineman (Sue) of Lebanon, and Greta C. Below of Morrisville. Henry Below also had two sisters; Freda and Lena Below, and one brother; Ernst H., all of Germany. Memorial services were held at the First Presbyterian Church of Morrisville.

Luckily, Henry had made a will, September 29, 1959, appointing Ernst H. as trustee. Under the terms of the will the business, known as Pennsbury Pottery, was to be left in trust for his wife (Lee) and their three children. According to the terms of the trust, the business was to be sold at the time of his wife's death. All proceeds were to be divided equally among the children and grand-children. After a long illness, Lee Below passed away, on December 12, 1968. It has been said, "she was a real hard worker, spent many hours, trying to keep the pottery business solvent." She was 63 years old at the time of her death. In May of 1971, after the demise of his mother, Ernst H., acting as trustee and executor, fulfilled the terms of his father's will. The land was disposed of (2,207 acres) for $100,000. This information is recorded in Deed Book 1997-474 at the Bucks County Courthouse. At this period in time this area, including the Below home, is occupied by a printing company.

After the death of Henry Below, Ernst and his mother continued to operate the Pottery which prospered for a few more years. When the Below family opened the business, in late 1950, the operation began with only sixteen or seventeen employees. It has been reported a few joined them from the Stangl Pottery. They also employed local housewives and young girls who were taught the trade. Some became adept enough to work as decorators. Incidently, Greta Below never worked at the Pottery.

Here are excerpts from several interesting interviews with former employees who revealed considerable information and confirmation of facts about the Pottery and it's products.

Alma Roberts—Worked from 1957 until the closing of the Pottery; then transferred to Glen View, and then to the Pennington Potteries. She was a decorator who painted the colors on the

An 11" "Boy and Girl" Plate without primary colors.

An 11" Plate with "Boy and Girl" pattern. Lee Below original.

5½'' left of a pair of Western Tanager #104. Signed B.S. Betty Shepard.

4'' Gold Finch #102. Signed B.S. Betty Shepard.

designs. She was also in charge of some the productions and assisted in creating some of the designs that were a team effort.

Betty Shepard—An artist who was in charge of the decorating department, and is credited with finishing many of the beautiful all white birds. After the Pottery closed, in 1970, she gained employment at the Lewis Brothers Pottery in Trenton, New Jersey. At Lewis Brothers, she and another ex-Pennsbury employee, Edith Guilfoy, assisted them in operating their business. Edith Guilfoy related that some of the Pennsbury molds were used at Lewis Brothers, however, the name "Pennsbury" was removed from most of these molds. The glaze that was used was entirely different and was fired only one time, resulting in a thin and dull finish.

Jenny Hume—Worked in the glazing department spraying on the final finish. This job was accomplished entirely by hand since no machinery was used.

Edith Guilfoy—Started with Pennsbury in 1957 and continued until the Pottery closed. She worked as a finisher, smoothing articles when they were removed from the molds. After the closing of Pennsbury, at the age of 71, she transferred to the Lewis Brother Pottery and remained there for a little better than two years. Edith states: "I remember removing the name "Pennsbury" from the items and that the quality of merchandise, made at Lewis Brothers, was not of the same quality as that which was produced at the Pennsbury Pottery."

Evelyn Guilfoy—(Edith's daughter-in-law) was the first person, outside of the Below family, to work in the office when the Pottery opened in 1950. In addition to office work, she assisted wherever she was needed. Her employment was not continuous, as she took time off to have her children. Upon returning to the Pottery, she sometimes worked, along with her other duties, in the showroom with Lee Below. She relates: "Mr. Henry Below was his own salesman in the beginning. Later, he hired others that included Sue's husband, Sam Heineman."

Albert Delellis—Started with Pennsbury during the early years of operation. Later, he was promoted to the executive branch of the company. After Pennsbury closed, Mr. Delellis gained employment with the Ispanky Company and became vice-president. He is retired, but is retained as a consultant.

Names of other employees that worked for the Pennsbury Pottery are:

E.P. Alexander—Artist, sculptor and salesman. Also company representative at trade shows.
Mr. Dalkins
Dorothy Dreisbach
Mildred Franks
Ray Hartranft—Salesman. When Pennsbury closed, he became a salesman for the Stumar Company.
(Glen View Pottery).
Mr. House—Salesman. Company representative at trade shows.
Violet Kanivrael—V.K. or K. Artist.
Jean McComber—J.M. Artist.
Dorothy (Dot) Parker—D.P. Artist.
Eleanor Purcell—E.P. Artist.
Ida Thatcher
Mr. Tiedeken—Salesman. Company representative at trade shows.
Esther Titus—E.T. Artist.
Lydia Schermerhorn—L.S. Artist.
George Schnell
Kathryn Strine—Office worker.

In what capacity some of these employees worked is unknown. Research revealed a few artist's initials, but not their full names or what their official duties were.

A.P., J.R., P.F.C., R.B., R.D.

Business improved steadily and, by 1960, the company had forty-one people in the work force. By 1963, the employee count had reached forty-six. This information was obtained from the Pennsylvania Directory of Industries. Evidently, by 1966, the pottery business began to slacken as the employee count had dropped to only twenty-nine. Between 1967 and the Pennsbury closing date (1970), several items were eliminated from the production line, probably due to lack of sales. The Pottery became a victim of these dwindling sales, as well as rising costs, a problem plaguing the majority of contending American Potteries. The cause of this demise was the heavy competition from Japan and Europe, which was flooding the American market with ceramic ware at a much cheaper price. Even prior to the mid-fifties large operations, such as Rookwood, Roseville, Weller, and many of the smaller, well known

Marsh Wren #106. 6½" tall. Signed K. Violet Kanivrael.

Blue Jay #108. 10½" tall. Very similar to Stangl .....* Blue Jay. Fully signed D. Parker.

"999..." 1891, impressed Alexander. Artist signed "S", Sue Below.

A 7½" x 4" "tulip" Dresser Tray with pastel shades. Signed E.T., Esther Titus.

Potteries, began to feel the pinch and were forced to close. These closings were not due to poor management, but rather to extenuating circumstances beyond their control.

In the late 1960's, the Pennsbury management made every effort to keep the enterprise operating on a profitable basis. However, their debt was constantly increasing and finally, all efforts failed. In the will and testament of Lee Below, she desired all her real and personal property to be sold and the money used to defray the debts of the business. At the time of her death, she was residing at her home, next to the Pottery, located on Olde Tyburn Road. The signature on her will is: Lee Elfrieda Below. By the time her estate was settled, the Pennsbury Pottery was no longer in existence, having filed for bankruptcy on October 29, 1970, in the United States District Court for Eastern Pennsylvania. Consequently, all production ceased. An auction was held, at the Pennsbury Pottery, at 10 A.M. on December 17, 1970. The following record, of the auction, appeared in the Courier Times, on December 18, 1970, reported by an on the scene staff writer, Mr. Zachary Stalberg. Only the interesting facts of Mr. Stalberg's report will be mentioned here.

The auction took a little more than five hours, with a crowd of several hundred people expected. However, the number that participated was a lot smaller. The piecemeal bids, from dealers and collectors, amounted to $23,715.80. It should be noted that before the start of the actual bidding, a Mr. Ray Gold of Conshohocken, and two associates, offered $30,000 for the entire lot. Consequently, they were awarded the complete contents. Not included in the contents were the buildings from which the business operated, the production plant and the retail showroom that was erected in 1964. The auctioneer was A.J. Pione, of Affiliated Auctioneers of Philadelphia. He thought the crowd was, "A good one." Ernst Below, later on during the day, stated: "There was talk of an attempted merger that failed. It's a sad day." What type of merger he was speaking of is unknown. A meeting of their creditors, was held in Philadelphia the following day and proceeds, from the auction, were divided. At the auction, catalogs were stacked high and free for the taking.

The final blow came at 5:59 P.M. on April 18, 1971. Ernst Below, who was residing next door to the Pottery, noticed that the pottery building was on fire. He immediately sounded the alarm.

Responding to the call were over 130 firemen from Falls Township, Fairless Hills, Levittown, Morrisville and Tullytown. Information concerning the fire was obtained from the Courier Times, written by staff writer Joseph Grimm. He stated: "The fire evidently started in the middle of the three building complex and, eventually, consumed the entire retail store that fronted on Olde Tyburn Road."

Thus, another sorrowful ending for another important American Pottery.

A 6½" Rare Pennsbury Wall Pocket signed LE. From the collection of Esther Keller. Photo by Keller.

Rooster and Hen. White leghorn. Company name.

Rooster and Hen, delft blue. Company name.

Rooster and Hen, dark brown and white. Collection of Joyce Smalley.

Rooster and Hen, Nutmeg brown and tan. Company given name.

Rooster and Hen, light brown and white with red combs. Marked: Rooster—P202-3. Hen—P201-3.

Rooster and Hen, brown and yellow. Note the pink on Hen's back.

Pennsbury Pottery Birds

One of the first products to be introduced, by the Pennsbury Pottery, was a line of birds. It's a reasonable presumption that this was one of Henry's pet projects. These birds are very similar to those produced at the Stangl Pottery, in their detail, coloring, shapes and glazes. The number of birds made at Pennsbury, was far less than the number produced by the Stangl Company. Perhaps the reason for this is that Stangl made birds for a longer period of time. A person can easily mistake one for the other, without first looking at the company mark. It has been reported, Pennsbury ceased general production of the birds sometimes during the mid-fifties. However, a limited number of birds were made after the mid-fifties, but by special order only. The three birds, dated "Spring 1965," that are included in this book, are examples of such a special order and are of excellent quality. The women who worked at the Pennsbury Pottery, related: "Pennsbury birds were never sold in the salesroom." Evidently, as soon as a quantity of birds were produced, they were distributed, by the sales force, among the many shops that were engaged in the selling of Pennsbury merchandise.

After a constant inspection of the 1950 birds it appears that some of the final birds made, at that time, are not of the same fine quality in detail, beauty and color as those that were made earlier. These later birds (1950's) do have the Pennsbury name hand incised on the base, under the glaze, instead of the customary hand lettering found on the earlier variety, and are also sparsely decorated. The lettering, on the early type, are in colors of blue, brown or black. Some molds were changed slightly from time to time, with the foliage removed or placed differently. However, the numbers remained the same. One such example is the Blue Jay, where a large leaf is

10½'' Blue Jay #108. Signed D. Parker.

applied on the front of the stump. On another model, the leaf is applied on the back side of the stump.

The largest of the Pennsbury birds are the eleven and one-half inch rooster and the ten and one-half inch hen. Several color schemes were utilized, such as cobalt blue on white, all white with red combs, brown on yellow, brown on cream, brown on pink, brown on white, green on white and various other multi-colors. It has been reported that there were as many as twenty or more different combinations of color and shade. A 1967 Pennsbury price sheet shows seven different sets of rooster and hen still available to their customers.

Multi-Color, Hen and Rooster

The numbers appearing on the Pennsbury song birds begin with 101—the Crested Chickadee. It has not been determined how many numbers were utilized, since no definite records have been located concerning numbers. The highest number discovered, thus far, in the song bird series is 123, assigned to the Barn Swallow.

The Hen and Rooster sets and the Eagle pieces were assigned a 200 series number. The Hen is numbered P 201 and the Rooster P 202. An additional number was attached to denote the color of decoration. For example: P 201-3 and 202-3 denote a white and brown set. Later, invoices indicate that the rooster and hen were given the numbers 127 and 128 respectively. The only ones found, thus far, with numbers on the base, are the 200 series. Why two different series of numbers were used is unknown.

Three sizes of spread Eagle plaques were produced using the sculptured method; the six and one-half inch, the twelve and one-half inch, and the large twenty-two inch, all measured from wing tip to wing tip. There is also a sculptured Eagle figure that measures six and one-half inches high, by six and one-fourth inches wide, in the sitting position, with partially raised wings. These pieces were also assigned a 200 series number—212, 213, 214, and 215 respectively. No artist signatures or initials have been found connected with the Eagle pieces. Eagle bookends were also made using the same mold as the figural (215)—in both green and all white. The company also presented the Eagles mounted on wood as well as free standing.

Several varieties of birds, made on the same molds, which are named and numbered, were also made without the name and number, but decorated differently, apparently to change the type or style. For example: The Wren, number 106, is decorated in the colors of the Marsh Wren, while the one with no number is decorated in the style of the Carolina Wren. Number 123, the Barn Swallow, has been discovered in several different versions. The earliest ones marked in color, are decorated in two or three color combinations. These are further embellished with leaves on the stump-like pedestal. On the revised or late model, the foliage has been removed and the tail shortened somewhat. These are marked Pennsbury and are also numbered and incised by hand under the glaze. The later birds are sparsely decorated. One of these later birds has been found in all blue, presumably to represent an Indigo Bunting. Another has been located in all yellow, very similiar to the Stangl Canary. Even though every variety of Pennsbury bird was decorated in colors, a limited number of these identical birds were duplicated in stark white and light ivory. These birds, in all white or ivory glaze, are exceptionally well sculptured and show fine detail. Collectors should consider these very rare. Many are initialed by Betty Shepard (B.S.). The following birds have been documented with name and number.

101—Crested Chickadee. (First bird issued). "Special order" model dated, Spring 1965.

102—Gold Finch. "Special order" model dated, Spring 1965.

103—Blue Bird.

104—Western Tanagers. Made in pairs. Left and right.

105—Scarlet Tanagers. Early model is dark red with black wings. Later type is pink with dark brown wings.

106—#1 Wren. Some birds are marked Marsh Wren.

#2 Wren. Unnumbered bird decorated in the mode of the Carolina Wren.

#3 Wren. Identical mold with impressed mark. Color is all tan with black dashes and stripes.

#4 Wren. All white with no decoration. All Wrens are on the same mold and have a tall pedestal.

107—Gnat Catcher.

108—Blue Jay. Almost identical to the Stangl Blue Jay.

109—Small 3" Wren.

4" Pair Crested Chickadees #101. Bird on right marked "Spring 1965". Signed PFC. Left bird signed K. Violet Kanivrael.

"Gold Finch" #102. Left: signed K. Right: signed P.F.C. Spring 1965.

4" Blue Bird #103. Signed K. Violet Kanivrael.

#104 Western Tanagers left and right. Both signed J.R. and L.S.

5½'' tall Scarlet Tanager #105. Early version. Hand marked. Dark red with black wings. Reverse side.

Wren 6½'' tall #106. Similar to Carolina Wren. Signed D.P. Dorothy Parker.

Scarlett Tanagers #105. Left: early model. Right: late model.

6½'' Marsh Wren #106. Signed B.S. Betty Shepard.

110—Nut Hatch.

111—Chickadee.

112—Magnolia Warbler. "Special order" model dated, Spring 1965.

113—Red Start.

114—Wood Duck.

117—Humming Bird Candle Holders (pair). Left and right.

119—Humming Bird.

120—Cardinal.

8" Eagle bookend.

22" Eagle plaque #P214. Collection Joyce Smalley.

Pair of Eagle bookends.

12½'' Eagle plaque #P213.

6½'' Gnat Catcher #107. Signed B.S. Betty Shepard.

6½'' Eagle plaque #P212. Collection Joyce Smalley.

6½'' two varieties of Gnat Catchers #107. Left bird not signed. Right bird signed J.M. Jean McComber.

10½'' Blue Jay #108. Signed B.S. Betty Shepard.

122—Audubon's Warbler.

123—Barn Swallow.
Birds with no documented number:

Ring Neck Pheasant. (In pairs) "Special Order" only.

Quail. (In pairs) "Special Order" only.

Sparrow
- Humming Bird—with flower blossom.
- Hawk—
- Eagle—with raised wings.

Domestic Ducklings (pair). Two poses—sitting and standing. Finished in white or yellow.

Large Ducks were also produced.

Rooster—P202 (127)

Hen—P201 (128)

The Rooster and Hen generally do not carry a number. Those that have been seen with a number are marked P 201 (hen) and P 202 (rooster). An additional number, after the P 201 and P 202, designates the color. Evidently, numbers 127 and 128 are invoice numbers.

The sizes, of the various song birds, will vary from about two and one-half inches to about ten and one-half inches in height, excluding the Ring Neck Pheasant which is larger in size. The birds are always marked, with the name of the Pottery, on the underside of the pedestal. Some are marked with a number, the name of the bird, the initial of the artist, and a few "1965 Special" birds are dated. Occasionally, the entire name of the artist will appear on the piece.

3½" pair of Nut Hatch #110. Right: signed D.P. Dorothy Parker. Left: signed K. Violet Kanivrael.

Chickadee #111. 3½" tall. Signed L.S. Lydia Schermerhorn.

#112 Magnolia Warbler. Left: signed K. Right: signed P.F.C. Spring 1965.

3" Wren, two versions. Brown bird signed L.S. #109.

#113 Red Start 3''.

10'' Woodchuck #114. All white.

10'' Wood Duck #114 facing right. Signed K Violet Kanivrael.

Hummingbird Candlesticks, 5''. #117.

3½'' Hummingbird #119. Signed B.S. Betty Shepard.

Cardinal #120, 6½'' tall. Signed K.

Left: #120 Cardinals. Signed R.B. Right: signed V.K. both 6½''.

4'' Audubon's Warbler #122. Signed J.R. unknown.

6¼'' Barn Swallow #123.

#123 Barn Swallow. 6¼''. Signed E.P. Eleanor Purcell.

Barn Swallow #123. Late version in yellow, similar to the Stangl ......* Canary, sparsely decorated. 6½'' tall.

Left: Barn Swallow #123. Right: Cardinal #120. Signature: B.S. Betty Shepard. Collection: Esther Keller.

Barn Swallow #123. Late version in blue is very similar to the Indigo Bunting also sparsely decorated. 6½'' tall.

6½'' Pair of Ducklings. Handmarked Pennsbury.

Pennsbury Pottery Line Names

Most of the Pennsbury designs are very reminiscent of the carved technique that was used at the Stangl Pottery. However, a few articles were produced in high or bas-relief molds. What makes this intriguing ware so popular, with collectors, is it's vast variety of forms and designs as well as the diversified characteristics of the creations.

The finish on Pennsbury pottery entailed two firings. First, the green ware (soft state) was washed or sponged with a brown stain or paint, allowed to dry and then fired. Finally, soothing, complimentary and appropriate colors were added in the proper places and then dried. After the colors were dried on the article, it was sprayed with a transparent glaze that is very seldom found crazed. After applying the glaze, the item was dried again and refired. Occasionally, articles were finished without the addition of the primary colors, resulting in solid tan or brown, and sometimes trimmed with dark brown borders. Some designs were further enhanced by adding enameled colors on top of the glaze. The background color, on Pennsbury pottery, varies from a light tan to a dark brown. The difference in color results from the density of the stain that was sponged on the body, of the piece. This background, with the beauty of handcrafted ware, and the blending of the complimentary colors, is the distinguishing characteristic of most of these charming creations, and are easily recognizable at a glance. Incidently, not every piece of Pennsbury bears the brown background, even though this is their mark of recognition. Other colors were used, but in a much lesser quantity. This will be discussed later in the book. Pennsbury pottery is made of a strong earthenware substance, fired at a high temperature. Several different clays were imported, mostly from Tennessee and Georgia.

"Slick-Chick 5½" Brown.

It may be worth noting, at this time, that many articles are drilled for hanging.

According to Evelyn Guilfoy, one of the next things to be introduced, after the garden birds, was a very unusual piece referred to, by the company, as the "Slick-chick." This is a very small yellow, blue or brown bird (chickadee type) perched atop a hollowed out gourd. The gourd, about five inches high, including the bird, was produced in mottled colors of green, blue or brown. These were the three main colors, though the color red was used sparingly. The little birds were placed on top of the gourds at various angles. However, these pieces proved very difficult to fire as the birds would sag. Collectors will notice that the little bird used atop the gourd, is the identical bird used on the little Pennsbury display sign. The "Slick-chick" is not always marked as it was mostly produced, in lots, for jobbers to resell. Also produced was a

"Slick-Chick" 5½". Note different color gourds and bird arrangements. Center Slick-chick marked Pennsbury.

"Slick-Chick" 5½" Blue bird.

"Slick-Bunny" 5½" tall. Marked Pennsbury. Paper label.

Pennsbury "Liberty Bell" 3½". Later, was produced by the Glen View and Pennington Potteries. Some have the paper label... others have not.

Group of Pennsbury Pitchers illustrating the six sizes created in this form. Left to right. 2½" "Amish Women", 3½" "Yellow Daisy", 4" "Red Rooster", 5" "Folkart", 6¼" "Amish", and 7¼" "Barber Shop Quartet".

Pennsbury 5" "Dutch Shoe". Some are decorated with hearts. Others have only the all brown finish. Some are marked... others are not.

"Slick-bunny"—perched atop an identical gourd, some with raised ears; others with the ears laid back. Some commemorative pieces (gourds) produced, were signed and dated. In speaking with Pennsbury employees—they claim that these novelties—(Slick-chick, Slick—bunny and the small Pennsbury display sign), can definitely be attributed to Lee Below. Liberty bells and rabbits were also created for outside distribution. Most of these unusual articles do not carry the Pennsbury Pottery trademark since they were produced, on special

Black Rooster Canister Set. Tea & Coffee 8" x 4½". Flour & Sugar 9" x 5¾".

"Black Rooster" vinegar and oil. Collection Joyce Smalley.

"Black Rooster" plate 10".

"Black Rooster" coffee pot 8".

"Black Rooster" tray 7½" x 5". Collection Joyce Smalley.

"Black Rooster" 6" tile.

"Black Rooster" plaque 4".

"Black Rooster" covered casserole 10¼" x 8¼". Collection Joyce Smalley.

"Red Rooster" cigarette box 5" x 4".

"Red Rooster" coffee mug.

"Red Rooster" 6" two cup coffee pot.

"Red Rooster" 6" plate. Note: The larger size plates have more background decoration.

4 cup "Red Rooster" tea pot. Collection Joyce Smalley.

6½" "Red Rooster" wall pocket.

"Red Rooster" candle holder 5".

Red Rooster relish tray five sections 14½'' x 11½''.
Collection Joyce Smalley.

''Red Rooster'' salt and pepper shakers 2½''.

''Red Rooster'' oval platter 11'' tall.

''Red Rooster'' 5'' footed compote.

order, to be resold. A dutch shoe was created, in the usual Pennsbury brown, about five inches long, sometimes marked Pennsbury. The dutch shoe was also produced for resale.

Along with the production of birds, tableware and many commissioned articles were produced. The first dinnerware line, for sale to the public, was the "Black Rooster" and the next was the multi-color "Red Rooster" pattern. Other patterns followed promptly, such as the "Folkart" line, created in the typical brown finish. Some pieces of Folkart have two confrontal birds, with foliage between them, while other pieces depict only one bird over heart and other various combinations of birds and foliage. These identical patterns were also used on solid white with cobalt blue decorations. This line is called "Blue Dowry," even though the decoration is the same as that on the brown Folkart ware. Sometime during the 1960's, the brown Folkart pattern was changed to "Brown Dowry" to correspond with "Blue Dowry." An early pattern was created known as regular "Toleware." This ware has a dark brown background, decorated with red and white fruit. Later, this identical ware was remade in white, with a brushed blue background, having the same all blue fruit decoration. This is known as "Delft Toleware." Alma Roberts, a decorator at Pennsbury, revealed that some white ware was also made, at still a later date, but only on special order. A dinner set with green rooster on white has been seen. She states: "Their principal product was the brown finished ware." A majority of the dinnerware lines are finished in the brown color. Apparently, full dinner sets, with all the serving pieces, were not too plentiful. The most prominent, of these sets, are the Red and Black Rooster. It may be worth noting, at this time, that Pennsbury purchased a supply of rooster place mats to accompany the rooster dinnerware pattern. Other dinnerware patterns are Folkart and two versions of the Hex. One version of the Hex has small heart-like designs added between the teardrop shape decoration. The second does not include the hearts between the teardrop design. This latter version was referred to, by the company, as "Pennsylvania Hex." Patterns will vary slightly, in some of the lines, due to the size and shape of the article. One may also notice that the colors used will vary on some designs and patterns. No doubt, this was done by the different artists who worked on the

"Red Rooster" 9" pie plate.

"Red Rooster" 11" Pennsbury "Chip and Dip". Collection Joyce Smalley.

"Red Rooster" tray 7½" x 5".

Pennsbury divided vegetable bowl 9½" x 6¼" "Red Rooster".

"Red Rooster" 6" tile.

"Red Rooster" covered cookie jar 8" tall.

"Red Rooster" egg cup 4" tall.

4" "Red Rooster" creamer and sugar.

6¼'' ''Red Rooster'' pitcher.

5'' ''Red Rooster'' pitcher. Note pale color.

5'' x 4'' ''Red Rooster'' butter dish. Collection Joyce Smalley.

#1 Pennsbury ''unfinished'' ''Angel'' Christmas plate after first firing.

''Red Rooster'' snack set. Collection Joyce Smalley.

''Folkart'' miniature pitcher 2½''.

#2 Pennsbury 'finished'' ''Angel'' Christmas plate after final firing.

10'' plate. Unfinished ''Folkart'' following first firing.

''Folkart'' butter dish 5'' x 4''.

''Folkart'' beverage mug 5''. One bird.

''Folkart'' pitcher 5''. Later called ''Brown Dowry''.

''Folkart'' beverage mug 5''. Two birds.

"Blue Dowry" pitcher 5". Same design as the "Folkart" line.

"Folkart" pie plate 9". Note: The dark color.

"Toleware" plaque 5" x 7" brown.

"Blue Dowry" plate 10".

"Delft Toleware" unusual design pitcher 5" obverse. Collection Joyce Smalley.

"Delft Toleware" 5" pitcher. Reverse side. Collection Joyce Smalley.

Delft "Toleware" canister, minus the lid.

Delft Toleware. Candlestick 3¾". Beverage Mug 4½".

Delft Toleware 9" bowl.

piece. The company allowed their employees to use their own ideas where colors were concerned.

Without a doubt, the most popular and sought after pieces, of Pennsbury, are the delightfully charming, whimsical and decorative wares that depict witty and pithy sayings. Other popular pieces are the Amish designs that include figures and various scenes. This particular type of art ware was made in a relatively small number of shapes, instead of complete sets. In some lines, only a limited number of forms were produced. For example, only two pieces have been discovered showing the "Family" pattern. These are a cake stand and an eleven inch plate. Some lines were produced in as many as ten or twelve different shapes such as mugs, pitchers, plates, plaques and various other items. The witty line called "Swallow the Insult", has only been found in three forms; a beer mug, a small tray and a round plaque. On the other hand, the "Amish" line consists of over a dozen articles, including the rare oil and vinegar bottles with the Amish head stoppers. Another rare item is the figural Amish head salt and pepper shakers in their all black garments. Other salt and pepper shakers were produced in the form of miniature pitchers, some with Amish figures and other painted patterns. Although some of these lines were limited, the company chose to assign a "line name and number" to each different design in their catalog. The primary number, under the item in the catalog, denotes the shape of the article while the second number designates the design or pattern.

The "Amish" pattern portrays a likeness of an Amish woman giving a pretzel to an Amish man who is holding a beer mug. A large double pretzel is shown on the reverse side of the mugs and pitchers. Other patterns, that include the

A "Hex" Coffee Mug, signed L.B.

A "Penna Hex" Cup and Saucer.

"Hex" Cup and Saucer.

A Six Cup "Hex" Coffee Pot. Note hearts in design.

Two Cup "Penna. Hex" Coffee Pot. Note there are no hearts in the design. Marked "Pennsbury Anna".

A 6" x 6" heart shaped "Hex" Candy Dish.

A 5" x 4" "Hex" Butter Dish. From the collection of Joyce Smalley.

A 2½'' "Hex" Miniature Pitcher. Note black paper label. From the collection of Joyce Smalley.

A 6¼'' "Hex" Pitcher.

A 6½'' "Hex" covered Casserole or Powder jar. From the collection of Joyce Smalley.

An 8'' "Hex Star" Ash Tray. From the Collection of Joyce Smalley.

A 6'' "Hex" Tile.

Amish people in the design, are Red Barn, Family, Harvest, Boy and Girl, and others in limited additions.

"Red Barn" shows a family of five, in front of a red barn, on the larger pieces. On the smaller pieces only two or three figures, on a fence, are depicted with the red barn pictured on the reverse side (cups and small pitchers). Large pieces consist of eight and ten inch plates, large pitchers, cookie jar etc. On invoices that have been seen, this pattern is referred to as "Farmer."

A 9'' "Hex" Bowl. From the Collection of Joyce Smalley.

Two 2½'' "Amish" Pitchers, decorated with a girl and a boy.

Salt and Pepper Shakers, decorated with "Amish" man and woman.

A 9'' Pie Pan. Version of the "Hex". From the collection of Esther Keller.

A 2½'' "Amish" Pitcher, decorated with an Amish woman.

A 3¼'' "Amish" Coffee Mug.

4'' "Amish" Sugar bowl and Creamer set, with Amish woman on the sugar bowl and Amish man on the creamer.

The reverse side of a 7½'' "Amish" Pitcher.

4'' "Amish" Sugar Bowl and Creamer set, with Amish man on the sugar bowl and Amish woman on the creamer.

A 4'' "Amish" Plaque.

Left: 7¼'' "Amish" Pitcher. Right: 6¼'' "Amish" Pitcher.

A 5'' "Amish" Beer Mug.

A 12" x 8" "Amish" Pretzel Bowl.

A 5" "Amish" Ash Tray.

9" "Bible Reading" Plate, without primary colors.

A 5" "Amish" Ash Tray with Pretzel and Root Beer added at the bottom.

An 8" Plate. "Chatting".

An 8" "Amish" Plate.

A 5" "Swallow the Insult " Beer Mug.

The reverse side of a 5" "Swallow the Insult" Beer Mug.

A "Swallow the Insult" Plaque, 5" x 7".

A 6" "Swallow the Insult" Plaque.

A "Red Barn" Pretzel Bowl, 12" x 8".

A Red Barn Cookie Jar. Reverse side.

The same Red Barn Cookie Jar. Obverse side.

A "Red Barn" Coffee Mug, 3¼". Signed L.B.

The reverse side of a 3¼" "Red Barn" Coffee Mug.

A "Red Barn" Pitcher, 6¼".

A "Red Barn " Pitcher, 6¼". Reverse side.

A 5" Red Barn Beverage Mug.

8" "Red Barn" plate.

A 14½" "Red Barn" relish Tree. from the collection of Joyce Smalley.

An 11" Special Pennsbury "Family" Plate made expressly for Henry Below by his wife Lee. From the collection of Esther Keller. Photograph, Esther Keller.

The reverse side of the special 11" "Family" plate. "Made for HB, March 11, 1956. Pennsbury Pottery LB."

11" Plate. "Family". From the collection of Joyce Smalley.

The Red Barn is a Lee Below creation and many pieces are initialed by her.

"Family" was introduced in the spring of 1956 and is also a Lee Below innovation. She presented an eleven inch plate to her husband (Henry) at the time. On the reverse of this plate is incised the caption, along with a heart, "Made for HB, March 11, 1956—Pennsbury Pottery LB." This design shows an Amish family of four, in silhouette, walking away together.

"Harvest" pattern displays an Amish couple carrying a laden holiday tray consisting of a pumpkin, turkey and other seasonal foods. There are two versions of the Harvest pattern, even though the difference is slight. On one, the turkey is deleted from the tray and the couple is walking forward, however, the man has his head towards the woman. The other version shows both people facing in the same direction. This is a Lee Below design, sometimes initialed LE or LB.

"Boy and Girl" pattern, an original by Lee Below, depicts a pair of bashful lovers, back to back, holding hands under a heart and foliage.

The remainder of the Amish decorated lines are self explanatory. These are: Chatting, Courting Buggy, Family Wagon, Walking to Homestead, Making Pie, Mother Serving Pie, Basket of Flowers, Picking Flowers, Bible Reading, Farm Scene, Kissing Over Cow, Horse

An 11" Cake Stand with "Boy and Girl" pattern.

An 8" "Harvest" Cookie Jar.

A 6" Plaque with "Boy and girl" pattern. Signed K.

An 11" "Harvest" Plate.

An 8" "Harvest" Pennsbury Plate.

A 5" Desk Basket, with "Two Women Under Tree".

A 5" "Tulip" Pennsbury Candleholder.. From the collection of Joyce Smalley.

4" Pennsbury Pitcher. "Tulip".

An 11" Plate with "Two Birds Over Heart".

An 11" Plate with "Pea Hen" over heart. From the collection of Joyce Smalley.

6" x 6" "Bird Over Heart", heart shaped Candy Dish.

A 5" "Fisherman" Beer Mug.

A 11" "Two Birds Over Heart" Cake Stand.

Reverse side of the 5" "Fisherman" Beer Mug.

A 5" "Fisherman" Plaque.

and Carriage, Two Women Under Tree, and Picking Apples, a Lee Below design, sometimes signed LEB or LB.

One of Pennsbury's most popular and nostalgic lines is the "Barber Shop Quartet." This design reveals four figures singing together. Shown below the four figures is a music measure accompanied by the words "Sweet Adeline."

A 9" "Dutch Talk" Bowl.

This decoration is found only on the large pieces, such as pitchers, plates, beer mugs and the large pretzel bowl. The smaller pieces, such as coffee cups and coasters, have only one member of the quartet shown. The quartet is always in the same position on the large pieces. The singers, from left to right, are Luigi, Olson, Schultz and Horowitz.

"Gay Ninety" discloses four figures (Two couples), standing at a bar, with their glasses raised in a toast. Inscribed below is the caption, "Here's Looking At You." Their clothing is that of the period. On the small coffee cup, only two people are shown with their glasses raised. No caption accompanies the piece. On some pitchers, one couple is shown on the obverse and one couple on the reverse, with no caption.

The "Eagle" line depicts the patriotic eagle in the form of the national emblem of the United States. This line is a favorite among many collectors. A decorative red and black shield is also depicted on the reverse side of the pitchers and mugs and on the front of the 12" x 8" pretzel bowls.

"Dutch Talk" has dutch sayings scattered about the article, with small dutch emblems, interspersed in the arrangement. This pattern is rare and extremely scarce. Listed are these saying."

1. I'm Fermixed and Ferhexed.
2. Go Pump Me a Drink.
3. Outen The Light.
4. Throw The Cow Over The Fence Some Hay.
5. My, You Look Good In The Face.
6. Kissen Wares Out, Cooking Don't.
7. Borrowing Makes For Sorrowing.
8. Bump! The Bell Don't Make.
9. Her Corns Ouch Her Somethin Wonderful.
10. Comb Yourself Onct, Your All Stubbly.

A 7¼" "Barber Shop Quartet" Pitcher. From left to right: Luigi, Olson, Schultz, Horowitz.

A 5" "Quartet" Coaster with the face of Schultz.

A 5" "Quartet" Coaster with the face of Horowitz.

A 5" "Quartet" Coaster with the face of Olson.

A 5" "Quartet" Coaster with the face of Luigi.

A 3¼" "Quartet" Coffee Mug with the face of Schultz.

Obverse side of a 5" "Barber Shop Quartet" Beer Mug. Left to right: Luigi, Olson, Schultz, Horowitz.

A 3¼" "Quartet" Coffee Mug with the face of Luigi.

Reverse side of the same mug.

A 3¼" "Quartet" Coffee Mug with the face of Olson.

12" x 8" Pretzel Bowl "Quartet". Left to right: Luigi, Olson, Schultz, Horowitz.

Obverse of a 5" "Gay Ninety" Beer Mug.

A 12" x 8" "Gay Ninety" Pretzel Bowl.

Reverse of the same mug.

Obverse of a 7¼'' "Gay Ninety" Pitcher.

Reverse of the same pitcher.

A 3¼'' "Gay Ninety" Coffee Mug.

5'' "Gay Ninety" Coaster or Plaque. From the collection of Joyce Smalley.

A 7½'' x 5'' "Eagle" Cigarette Tray, sculpted in bas relief.

A 5'' "Eagle" Beer Mug.

A 3¼'' "Eagle" Coffee Mug.

A 3¼'' "Eagle" Coffee Mug with reverse side showing Shield.

A 7½'' x 5½'' "Eagle" Plaque sculpted in high relief.

Obverse of a 5¼'' "Eagle" Pitcher.

Reverse of the same pitcher showing the shield.

A 12'' x 8'' ''Eagle'' Pretzel Bowl. Note the dark shades.

A 5'' tall ''Eagle'' Desk Basket sculpted in high relief.
3½'' x 5''. Cigarette Box with applied Eagle. Collection of Joyce Smalley.

An 8'' ''Eagle'' Plate. From the collection of Joyce Smalley.

A 6" Pennsbury Plaque with "Mother Serving Pie". Signed K. Note dark background (possibly the antique finish).

A 6" Pennsbury Plaque "Mother Serving Pie". Note the light background and dark dress. From the collection of Esther Keller. Photo by Keller.

A 5" ash Tray. Translated..."What's the matter? What hurts you?"

A 5" Ash Tray, translated... "Don't be so clumsy".

5" Ash Tray.

5" Ash Tray.

On the "Fisherman" line, the large articles portray two fishermen, in their fishing gear, with their catches. One man is holding a large fish while the other man, looking a little disgusted, holds a tiny catch. A swimming fish is depicted on the reverse side. On the small pieces, such as coasters, the swimming fish is pictured alone on the obverse side of the piece. These came in sets of four with different fish.

A few pieces were designed with flowers and birds. These lines are named Tulip, Two Birds Over Heart, and Bird Over Heart.

Pennsbury introduced a line of small octagonal trays, five inches by three inches. These are decorated with horses, birds and flowers, each incorporating a heart. These trays are copyrighted and are marked with the copyright circled "C" and the name Pennsbury.

A line of ash trays and hanging plaques were created, each with clever sayings in the native language or slang. Each piece is further embellished with appropriate drawings. The five inch ash trays are circular with three cigarette rests.

A 5" x 3" Copyrighted Octagonal Tray, "Crested Birds". From the collection of Joyce Smalley.

A 5" x 3" Copyrighted Octagonal Tray, "Horses".

4" Plaque. Collection of Joyce Smalley.

A 4" Plaque. Translated..."Falling down is having to get up again".

A 4" Plaque.

A 4" Plaque.

6" Plaque.

A 4" Rooster Plaque.

A 6" Plaque.

A 4" Pennsbury Plaque, "It's making Down". From the collection of Esther Keller. Photo by Keller.

A 6" Plaque.

A 6" Plaque, "Making Pie. Signed K. From the collection of Joyce Smalley.

A 6" Plaque, "Horse and Carriage". Signed K.

A 6" Plaque, "Walking to Homestead".

A 6" Plaque, "Kissing Over Cow".

A 6" Plaque, "Pea Hen".

A 6" Plaque, "Farm Scene". From the collection of Joyce Smalley.

A 6" Plaque, "Picking Flowers". Signed K. Note the light background.

A 6" Plaque, "Picking Flowers". Signed K. Note the dark background.

A 6" Plaque, "Basket of Flowers". Signed K. Note the dark background. From the collection of Joyce Smalley.

A rare Pennsbury Plaque "Neshaminy Woods", 7½" x 5½".

A "Neshaminy Woods" Letter Holder.

A 6½" x 6½" "Wall Pocket". Pink border and pink sails.

A 6½'' Rare Pennsbury Wall Pocket signed LE. From the collection of Esther Keller. Photo by Keller.

A 4'' Unusual Design Pitcher with ''Yellow Daisy'' pattern, circa 1959.

A 4'' ''Spatter'' Pitcher, pink on white. Signed H.B. From the collection of Phyllis Larson.

An Unusual Tray, 7½'' x 5'' ''tulip''. From the collection of Joyce Smalley.

A 5½'' Unusual Candle Holder ''Maypole Dance''. From the collection of Joyce Smalley.

An 11½'' "Neshaminy woods" Plate.

6½'' Wall Pocket with brown border. Signed L.E.

A 6½'' Wall Pocket without primary colors. Initialed LE, Lee Ehrlich Below.

A 10" "Bellows" Candy Box minus the lid. Eagle pattern.

A 10" "Bellows" shaped Wall Pocket with Eagle decor in high relief. Also comes in covered candy box. From the collection of Joyce Smalley.

A 6½" Wall Pocket with blue border.

A 6½" Wall Pocket with green border, signed L.E. From the collection of Joyce Smalley.

3¾" Rare Tumbler.

A 6½'' Rare Wall Pocket with pink border. From the collection of Joyce Smalley.

An 11'' Pennsbury Plaque with Church Facade. Pair #106 Wrens.

13½'' charger, ''St. George Slaying the Dragon''.

A 10'' Rare Pennsbury Scenic Plate. From the collection of Esther Keller. Photo by Keller.

6½'' Rare Wall Pocket trimmed in pink. Collection of Joyce Smalley.

The majority of the round plaques are four, five and six inches in size. The four inch size depicts the identical designs that appear on the ash trays.

The round six inch plaques display different moods. Some repeat the designs displayed on the Amish people decorated lines. Others have ingenuous drawings with pithy sayings. One excellent example of such a saying, found on one of these plaques, depicts a skunk with the adage, "Why Be Disagreeable, When With a Little Effort, You Could Be a Real Stinker." Collectors will notice that some of these plaques may have been sponged with lampblack or a thin coat of black paint, creating an extremely dark background, with some lighter than others. The girls who worked at Pennsbury mentioned an antique finish. This could possibly be what they were referring to. After examining such a piece, it creates the illusion of having been burned or aged in some form. However, this does not detract from it's appearance.

Pennsbury produced a four piece canister set, consisting of flour, sugar, coffee and tea. These pieces came equipped with wooden lids, topped with a rooster finial, one and three-fourths inches tall by two inches long. Sizes of the canister sets are of the usual varied type. The flour and sugar are 9" high and 5¾" in diameter. The coffee and tea measures 8" high and 4½" in diameter. The patterns are Red and Black Rooster, Folkart and Hex. Other patterns were made on request only. Invoices show the Rooster pattern was still available until the Pottery closed.

The 7" x 5" plaques were made in abundance and were used for all patterns and many commissioned pieces. One such plaque was the Colt Gun. Three have been seen, Double Action, Navy Model and Wells Fargo. These pieces used decals or stencils instead of the usual hand painted process.

The Pennsbury "Christmas" plate, for sale to the public at Pennsbury, was issued for only one year. This is the 1970 Stumar "Angel" plate. Later it was issued by the Glen View and Pennington Potteries, using the original markings. The name Stumar was the brainchild of Sidney Sachs, a jobber of Pennsbury products, and was coined from the first three letters of his son's names, Stuart and Mark. Lee Below designed the plate and it is marked, "LB Original" on the reverse side. Since Lee Below

A 1960 first issue Treetops Christmas Plate.

A 1961 Treetops Christmas Plate.

A 1962 Treetops Christmas Plate.

A 1964 Tree Tops Christmas Plate.

A 1963 Tree Tops Christmas Plate.

A 1965 Pennsbury Tree Tops Christmas Plate.

A 1966 Tree Tops Christmas Plate.

A 1967 Treetops Pennsbury Plate.

A 1968 Pennsbury Tree Tops Christmas Plate.

A Tree Tops Christmas Plate, 1969.

The reverse side of the Treetop Plates.

A 5½" Candle Holder with Holly.

A 5½" Candle Holder with Holly. From the collection of Joyce Smalley.

An 11" Chip and Dip. From the collection of Joyce Smalley.

A 5" Compote with Holly.

A 5" Compote with Holly.

was deceased two years prior to the release of the 1970 Stumar Christmas plate, indicates that some designs were in the creating stage for several months or longer before they were released.

Some Christmas merchandise was decorated for the normal Christmas trade, while other articles were made especially for customers who commissioned them for their own employees and friends as gifts. The Hershey Chocolate Company of Hershey, Pennsylvania, commissioned at least one Christmas plate. On the reverse side of the plate is "Hershey Yuletide Plate", however, no date is shown. It is unknown whether further Yuletide plates were comissioned by Hershey, or how many of these special plates were made.

One line of Christmas plates were designed for Mr. and Mrs. Douglas K. Porteous, of Paoli, Pennsylvania. These first ten plates, by Pennsbury, are titled "Tree Tops" or "Treetops" (spelled both ways), dated 1960 through 1969, and are identical, in size, to the Stumar "Angel" plate. The dates are tucked into the design in an appropriate place. The wording on the front of the plate is "Christmas Greetings," incised at the top and "Tree Tops" or "Treetops" at the bottom. The reverse shows the name Mr. and Mrs. Porteous, with their address inscribed on the edges. The Pennsbury mark is shown in the center. Tree Tops is the name of the estate where the Porteous' resided. They no longer reside there, since she is deceased and he makes his home in Florida. Alma Roberts, who was in charge of overseeing the Tree Tops plates, related, "I remember Mrs. Porteous coming, with her chauffeur, every year to order her plates. She requested a relatively large number, each year, and sent them out as Christmas cards." The Porteous' commissioned a series of fourteen plates in all, however, since the Pennsbury Pottery closed in 1970, the remaining four plates (1970 through 1973) were produced by the Glen View Pottery.

At Christmas time each year, the Below family presented their employees with gifts of pottery. For several years, the Tree Tops plates were given after obliterating all the wording except "Christmas Greetings" and the date. Not all workers received the same thing, however, the gifts they did receive came from regular stock; such as candle sticks, plates, plaques, cigarette trays and others. Many of these gifts were initialed and dated.

11" x 8" Ship Plaque. "Charles W. Morgan" "The Bark". Collection of Esther Keller.

"Stourbridge Lion", 1829.

The Pennsbury Pottery "family" was very close. When there was an event to celebrate, such as a birth, an eleven inch plate was designed and each worker signed it, in it's green stage, with his or her given name. Evelyn Guilfoy owns such a plate that was designed by Lee Below and given to Evelyn when she had her first child, in September of 1951. The plate is signed by seventeen co-workers, including Lee Below. This was the total force of employees at that period in time.

A limited number of articles were molded in high relief instead of the carved designs. These are the "Railroad" plaques or trays, "Ship"

"John Bull", 1831. Gold tab on reverse.

A "Lafayette" 1837.

plaques or trays, a few "Eagle" and other line pieces. The railroad plaques are seven and one-half by five and one-half inches in size. There is a series of nine, each picturing a different and celebrated old locomotive. The following are the names of these locomotives.

"Star"—Central R.R. of New Jersey. 1870. Reported to be the first one made in this series of nine.

"Tiger"—Pennsylvania R.R. 1856

"General"—Western and Atlantic R.R. 1855

"John Bull"—Camden and Amboy R.R. 1831

"999"—New York Central and H.R.R.R. 1891

"C.P. Huntington"—Central Pacific R.R. 1863

"Lafayette"—Baltimore and Ohio R.R. 1837

"Camelback"—Philadelphia and Reading R.R. 1880

"Stourbridge Lion"—Delaware and Hudson R.R. 1829 This was the final railroad plaque produced.

Impressed on the reverse, of some of these plaques, is the name "Alexander." Some have a gold label, on the reverse, relating the history of the locomotive that is shown on the obverse side. Below this label is a tab with the name E.P. Alexander, Yardley, Pennsylvania. He was the designer and sculptor of these plaques and possibly the ship plaques as well, since they are so similar in workmanship. Two of the (gold label) tabs reveal the following histories of the "John Bull" and the "C.P. Huntington." "The John Bull was the first locomotive to run in New Jersey and is the oldest original engine preserved in the United States today. Built in England at the works of George and Robert Stephenson, it was shipped, dismantled, to Bordertown; assembled by Isaac Dripps and first run on November 12, 1831." "The C.P. Huntington was built by Danforth, Cooke and Co., Patterson, New Jersey in 1863, and was one of the pioneer locomotives of what is now the Southern Pacific, which came around Cape Horn by sailing ship. In service for many years since 1864, it is preserved today at the Sacramento station."

The "Ship" series consist of eight different sailing ships and one steamship. The size and shape of these plaques are very similar to those of the railroad plaques, however, some larger pieces were made. Listed are the names of these ships.

"Dreadnaught"

"Barkentine"

"Schooner"

"Raleigh"

"Lighting"

"Charles W. Morgan" "The Bark"

"Constitution"

River Steamboat "Mississippi" on the paddle wheel.

"Flying Cloud"—Date 1851. Two sizes of plaques.

Relating a bit of history concerning the clipper ship, Flying Cloud (1851-1874). It was one of the most famous among the swift ships that raced across the Atlantic and Pacific. Two hundred—twenty nine feet in lenght and carrying thirty five sails on it's mast, it was considered the fastest merchant ship of it's day. The Flying Cloud established a time record of eighty—nine days, sailing from New York to San Francisco, around Cape Horn, a distance of approximately 14,500 miles. This record was held for 135years (1854—1989), only to be broken by the sixty foot racing yacht "Thursday's Child." This same distance was accomplished in eighty days. The Flying Cloud was wrecked off St. Johns, Newfoundland, in 1874. It carried many adventurers during the California Gold Rush days.

Beginning in the early 1950's, a line of commemorative merchandise was made available to their customers. The Pennsbury Pottery did considerable amounts of this specialty work, even to making just one of an item, if so desired by a customer. Included were special plates for Christmas, wedding plates for the newlyweds, ash trays, beer mugs, coasters and many other desired articles, such as two sizes of personalized

9½" x 7" "The Flying Cloud". Dated 1851.

"General", 1855.

A "Tiger" 1856.

"C.P. Huntington", 1863.

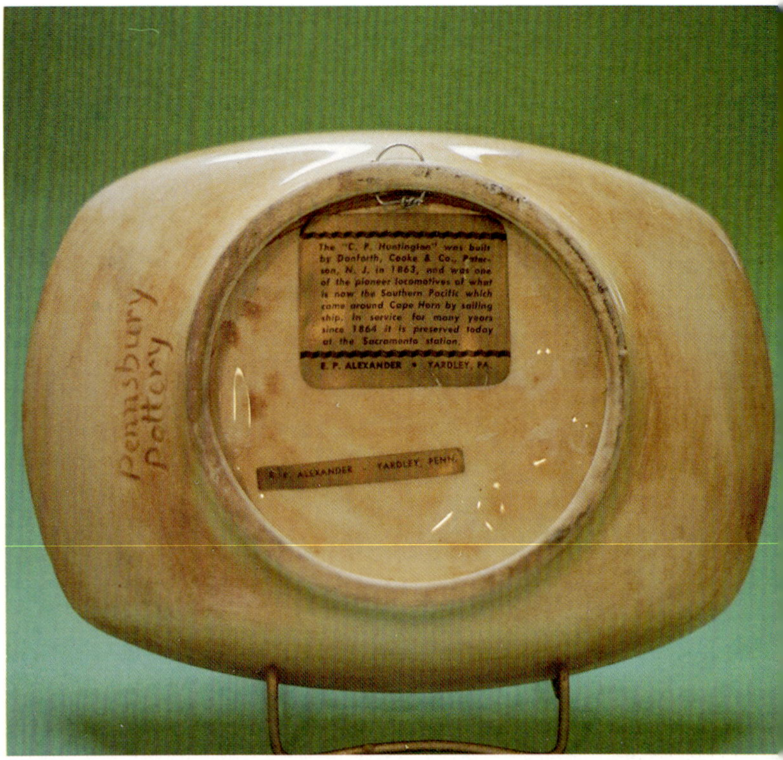

The reverse side of C.P. Huntington, showing gold tab.

"Star" 1870 First Plaque issued. Impressed Alexander.

7½'' x 5½'' Ship Plaque. ''Barkentine'' 1880. Collection of Joyce Smalley.

11'' x 8'' Ship Plaque. U.S. Frigate ''Constitution''. Collection of Joyce Smalley.

13½'' x 10¼'' ''River Steamboat''. Collection of Joyce Smalley.

4" Desk Basket. "Lafayette". Collection of Joyce Smalley.

A 5" National Exchange Club Desk Basket.

A 5" Pennsbury Commemorative Ash Tray, 1961.

A 4" "Pop's Half et already" Commemorative Plaque. Reverse caption, NFBPWC Philadelphia, PA 1960.

A 5" Doylestown Trust Co. Coaster, 1896-1958.

7¼" x 5¼" Tray. "Mayflower II" June 1957. Province Town, Massachusetts.

A 5" Commemorative Ash Tray.

An 8" Commemorative Plate, with a boat landing on the Delaware, 1966.

11" Commemorative Plate. "Turkey Hunt". Collection of Joyce Smalley.

An 8" Bucks County Week Commemorative Plaque, June 7-13, 1953. The river running through the scene is the Delaware. Sponsored by the Junior Chamber of Commerce.

An 8" Pennsbury Inn Ash Tray.

8" Commemorative Plaque United States Steel 1954

birth plates, one eight inch and one eleven inch. Special "Legal Eagle" mugs were made for attorneys, who were members of the Bucks County Bar Association, showing the name of the attorney and the date of his induction into the Association. The United States Steel commissioned an eight inch commemorative plate, each year, for at least nine years (1952—1960). The identical design was used every year, adding only a change of color and the date of the plate. In addition, other organizations; such as various railroads, insurance companies, clubs and churches commissioned commemorative articles. These special pieces included the organization's appropriate names and dates that were requested. The Pennsbury Pottery was always more than eager to please.

One of the most interesting and rare pieces made is a tray or plaque, designed for the occasion of the final running of the last steam locomotive operated by the Reading Railroad. This tray depicts the "Iron Horse Ramble" #2124, dated 1960. The tribute is printed on the reverse of the tray. This tray was produced in a limited number and was given to passengers participating in the final run of the locomotive. The trays were distributed boxed. Another extremely rare article, is a single plate that was made and presented to Walt Disney when he attended the opening of the Walt Disney School in Levittown.

Unexpected Pennsbury patterns and colors appear occasionally and will not be immediately recognized as a Pennsbury product without first looking at the company mark. Some of these patterns are abstract, incorporating birds (peahens) and flowers (tulips). Some articles are found designed with types of art deco; such as girls with flowers and other very unusual designs. On these unusual items, the colors are in shades of green, ranging from a very light shade to a dark olive—drab. Various shades of pink and rose were also used. However, the ones most often encountered are the green shades.

7¼" x 5¼" "Iron Horse Ramble". Commemorative Plaque. Reading R R.

Some of these unexpected patterns, with their unusual colorings, are the wall pockets, tiles, round plaques, plates small trays and various other odd pieces. The most popular variety of the wall pockets are all molded in one form, octagonal in shape, six and one—half inches in size. They are flat on the bottom and well balanced, and are suitable to set upright on a shelf or table, as well as hanging on a wall. Many different scenes will be found on these wall pockets and many are initialed on the front, LE, reputed to be the initials of Lee Ehrlich (Below). These initials will generally be found in the lower right—hand corner of the piece. Some wall pocketss were produced in the brown finish only, plus the scene, while others will have a colored border, such as green or pink. The ones with the pink are considered the rarest. Another type of wall pocket produced is the bellows. These are not as plentiful as the octagonal type, nor are they decorated in the same manner.

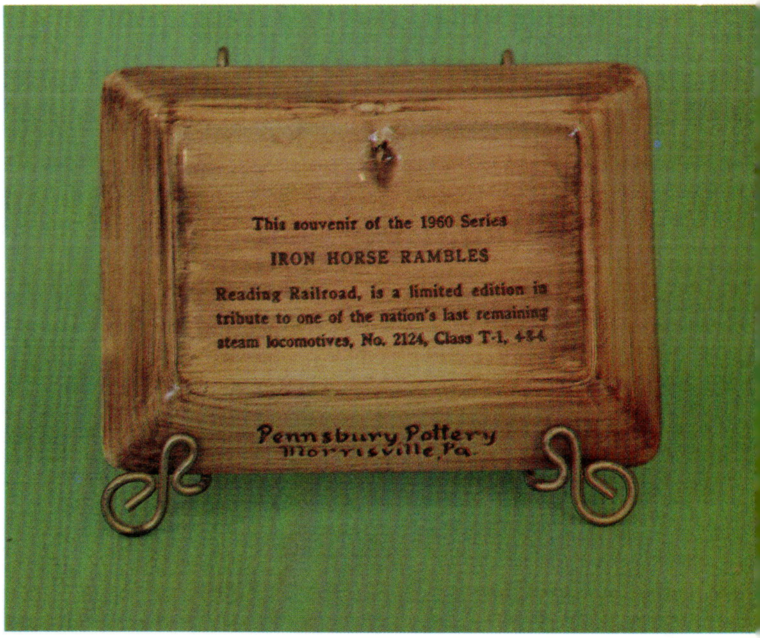

Reverse side of "Iron Horse Ramble" Railroad Plaque.

8½" x 5¼" Tray. Famous old landmark. Laurel Ridge.

A 7" x 6" Fidelity Mutual Life 75th Anniversary Commemorative Tray, 1955. Note rare plum color.

8½" x 5¼" Tray. Famous old landmark. Laurel Ridge.

A 5" Bucks County Fire Department Commemorative Mug, Honoring William Penn.

Reverse side of the same mug.

A 5" Plaque, "Washington Crossing the Delaware".

A 7½" x 5½" Railroad commemorative Plaque. Baltimore and Ohio R.R. Veterans, Philadelphia 1955.

A 7¼" x 5¼" Commemorative Tray from the N.E.A. Centennial 1857-1957. William Penn came to America in 1682 on the ship "Welcome".

Reverse side of above tray.

5" Ash Tray. Commemorative piece. Celebrated landmark. Summerseat. 1804-1954.

An 8" Golden Anniversary Rotary International Commemorative Plaque, 1954. District 265 Harry Simpson, Governor.

An 8" Church of the Redeemer Commemorative Tray, Longport, NJ. 1908-1958.

A 7½" x 5½" National Newark and Essex Commemorative Ship Plaque. Banking Company, 1804-1954.

A "Slick-chick" P.M.A.A. Commemorative piece. Pennsbury Pottery, 1967.

A 5" Commemorative Plaque, Groundhog Lodge #9 on the Deep Run.

Pennsbuty Novelties

A few novelty pieces were produced by Pennsbury. Most of these various articles are somewhat different in form than those mentioned here-to-fore.

Bread plates were offered in two forms; one eight inch round and one oval shape 6" x 9" verticle. Each plate is decorated in the identical manner, with a sheaf of wheat in the center. The familiar inscription, "Give Us This Day Our Daily Bread" appears around the rim of the plate.

Fish shape dishes were created in three forms; one round fish, one long fish and one small long fish. All are in the typical brown finish with the decoration in five or six different colors, making them appear very realistic. At this time, the dimensions of these three pieces are unknown.

Lamps were made and packed in kits for the customer to assemble. A suitable shade or chimney could be added according to one's own taste or desire. The lamps were molded in the shape of beer mugs, large pitchers and other cylindrical shape bodies that are about fifteen inches tall. The size, form and decoration of mugs and pitchers are the same as those in their regular stock of merchandise, except they are potted solid across the top. Pin-up wall lamps were also available, enhanced by using one of Pennsbury's six inch plaques and also by fitting it with a matching parchment shade. Finger candle holder lamps were included in the Pennsbury stock. All table lamps were drilled for the hardware, and wooden bases were included in the kits.

Oil and vinegar bottles were presented with the heads of the Amish man and woman used for stoppers. Inscribed on these bottles are pithy sayings. On the vinegar, "Vee Get Too Soon Old" and on the oil, "Undt Too Late Schmart." Other vinegar and oil bottles were also produced, but were decorated with the same designs as found on some of the dinnerware patterns, such as the red and black rooster. These bottles have the rooster finial for the stopper.

A few rectangular pen holders were produced, with a receptacle at the top, to hold the writing pen. Some are decorated with a molded eagle in bas-relief.

Other outstanding items, made by the Pennsbury Pottery, are nine inch pottery pie pans. Each plate or pan depicts one of the Amish figure patterns in the center, with sentimental inscriptions around the edge. Six of these scenes are, "Making Pie," "Boy and Girl," "Harvest," "Walking To Homestead," "Picking Apples," and "Mother Serving Pie." The Hex, Folkart and both Red and Black Rooster were also available.

A covered candy box, the same shape as the bellows wall pocket, was issued in the Eagle pattern. The lid does not cover the entire bottom, but is shortened at the narrow end. Also, an Eagle planter was produced in the same shape as the bellows wall pocket. All bellows pieces have the identical dimensions.

Banks were produced using the identical mold as the vinegar and oil bottles, decorated with a pig and inscribed with the caption, "Stuff Me." Banks were also made for the Hershey Chocolate Company in the form of Hershey

8" Bread Plate.

9" x 6" Bread Plate.

10" Small Long Fish #1102.

4½" set of Fisherman Coasters. Collection of Joyce Smalley.

A 7½" Pennsbury Lamp plus the hardware. From the collection of Esther Keller. Photo by Keller.

Wall or Pin-up Lamp, using 6" plaque with matching parchment shade with metal hardware. From the collection of Norman Haas.

7" Amish Line Vinegar and Oil Dispensers.

A 9" "Mother Serving Pie" Pennsbury Pie Pan.

When the Fragrance of Your Baking
Fills the House with Smells So Nice
We All Get That Natural Aching For
"Please, May We Have a Slice?"

A 9" "Walking To Homestead" Pennsbury Pie Pan.

When It's Time for Celebrating
Holiday's and Merry Making
Home We Go with Smiling Eyes
To Mom's Good Feast and Tasty Pies

A 9" Pennsbury "Pie Pan", "Picking Apples".

Apples Rosy, Shining Bright
On the Tree They are a Sight,
But Prepared into a Pie
They Delight Your Taste and Eye

A 9" "Boy and Girl" Pennsbury Pie Pan.

Whispered Words Beneath the Bower
Holding Hands at Some Late Hour
Usually Lead as You Well Know
To Raising Young Ones, Crops and Dough

A 4" Chocolate Brown Hershey Kisses Bank.

A 7" Bank.

A 14½" x 11½" Relish Tray with tulip pattern.

Pair "Rooster" Candle holders. 4". Marked Pennsbury. Unglazed bottoms.

Two sizes of "Amish" head Salt and Pepper Shakers.

Part of the five piece Spice Set, 3¾". Collection of Joyce Smalley.

kisses. However, these banks do not carry the Pennsbury mark. They were produced in both the chocolate brown and silver color or finish.

Relish trees or trays were made in the form of a Christmas tree or triangular shape, with either three or five compartments. These are fourteen and one-half inches tall and eleven and one-half inches across the bottom, with a stem protruding at the base. Various decorations were used, some with holly and others with scenes showing Amish figures (Red Barn pattern). The tulip was used extensively, mixed with other dutch designs. The tulip was very popular and used in many of the early and unusual pieces that Pennsbury produced. This pattern is also very hard to find.

Small figural hen and rooster candle holders, to accompany either the red or black rooster lines were produced. These are four inches in height, white, trimmed in multi-colors or black.

Other extremely rare items are the salt and pepper shakers molded in the form of the heads of an Amish man and woman, dressed in their all black native garb. These were made in two different sizes; two and one-fourth inches high and two and three-fourths inches tall. A larger base accounts for the extra one-half inch. Salt and pepper shakers were also made for the Hershey Chocolate Company. These are in the form of Hershey kisses. They do not carry the Pennsbury mark and were produced in both the chocolate brown and silver color or finish. As stated previously, some commissioned pieces do not have the Pennsbury signature as they were purchased for resale.

Pennsbury invoices include a five piece spice set in the rooster pattern and one in a dutch type design. Also listed is a pepper mill and matching salt shaker in the rooster pattern.

Six inch tiles, with various decorations, were marketed and placed in wooden frames. These are framed in panels, using two or three tiles, to hang in either vertical or horizontal position. Single tiles were also framed. In addition to the tiles being placed in frames, some were adhered to electrified metal warming plates.

Very unusual are the eleven inch personalized "Wedding" plates. The bride and groom could choose a plate, with a desired scene, then have

11" Pennsbury Wedding Plate with boy and Girl. Marked LB original. Sandra L. Ridge & Edward D. Dewees, married on the 18th Day of May in the year 1963.

An 8" Plaque "Pennsbury Manor". Note black label. From the collection of Joyce Smalley.

An 8" "Birth" Plate. Daniel George Prevcil, Born on the 10th Day of August in the year 1968.

A 7½" x 5" Colt 31 Caliber Novelty Tray. From the collection of Joyce Smalley.

2 quart rare Pennsbury Pitcher and Irish Coffee Mug decorated with decals and gold trim.

their names and date of marriage inscribed around the edge or rim of the plate. Several different center scenes were available to choose from. There are also personalized birth-plates, with several various center scenes to choose from. The names and date, of the event, would then be inscribed.

The Pennsbury Pottery produced an attractive small display sign (5'' W x 4½'' H), depicting the pottery name, with a tiny bird perched atop. One of the two types of birds used is of the identical mold that was used on the "Slick-chick" gourd; blue, yellow or brown. The position of these birds, on top of the sign, will vary as they do on the gourd.

A very unusual clock was created by Pennsbury, in their early years, approximately six inches square. These are decorated with full figures, in full relief, of a colonial lady on one side of the time piece and a gentleman on the other. She is dressed in pink and blue and he is wearing tan and blue. The background of the clock case is white with green scrolls. The face of the clock is small; about two inches in diameter. One of these fine pieces is in the collection of

Pennsbury Pottery 5'' x 4½'' display signs.

Rare Green Rooster sugar bowl and plate.

Edith Guilfoy, and she related: "It was given to me, by Mrs. Below, in the early years of operation." It has been reported that Pennsbury, during the initial years of production, also made free standing figurines, also animal figurals (a horse has been seen). Since no figurines or figurals have been seen, outside of the horse, one may assume the production did not last very long. They were probably too difficult to make and broke easily.

Some pieces of Pennsbury, such as pie pans and tureens, came equipped with fitted metal racks. Also, a few of the plates were produced with metal rims and loop handles.

Articles, referred to as "Spatter-ware," were produced in pink on white, brown on white and blue on white. This ware is very similar to a line that was produced by the Stangl Company, in their final years of operation. The pattern is also referred to as "Homespun," by some collectors. No pieces have been discovered, incorporating designs of any kind, other than the random spatter. These are small pitchers, one of each color, about the same size as the cream pitcher that accompanies the regular Pennsbury sugar bowl. Also, miniature size pitcher salt and pepper shakers have been seen in this design. Other colors, besides the pink, blue or brown, may exist, such as the black, which has been reported to have been seen.

Hanging plaques were made baring a facsimile of a United States coin. Buffalo nickels and Mercury dimes have been seen.

Electrified Warming Plate 6'' x 6''. Picking Apples, signed L.B.

An 8'' Mercury Dime Plaque.

Both marked Pennsbury but note indistinct design on left pitcher, no doubt Lewis Brothers. Right is Pennsbury.

Both marked Pennsbury, but note poor quality of left pitcher, no doubt Lewis Brothers. Right is Pennsbury.

Pennsbury Look-alike, "Oil and Vinegar". Lewis Brothers, poor quality...unmarked.

Pennsbury Pottery Marks/Lewis Brothers Pottery

The marks on Pennsbury pottery will vary, from one article to another, depending on the person who signed the piece or the artist who sculptured the molds. The earliest pieces are all signed by hand, at the time they were decorated, with either a small brush or some sort of soft tipped pen. Most pieces are signed in colors of blue, brown or black. Occasionally, a piece will be found that is signed in red. The signatures, on the molds, are in several styles of script and are in various sizes, some quite large, depending on the size of the article. Some Pennsbury marks will be found either hand incised or stamped. A number of the earliest pieces were finished without glazing the bottoms and sometimes the marks are faded quite badly and might be missed, unless they are scrutinized closely.

Occasionally, articles will be found marked Pennsbury Pottery with the word "Anna" beneath this mark. The signature Anna is really an abbreviation for Penna. or Pa., and was used by natives in this specific area of Pennsylvania. Collectors will notice that the word Anna has a fancy "A" on the signature. This particular type signature is only found on some of the "Pennsylvania Hex" pattern pieces. It is very unusual, but a few pieces of Pennsbury pottery will be found that entirely escaped being marked. Some of these unmarked pieces, known to be Pennsbury, were pieces that the workers made, for themselves, to take home for their own use. Miniature articles were never marked with the full Pennsbury name, due to the small size. In some cases, only the single letter (P) was used, or their small black paper label was utilized. It is indeed a rarity to find a piece of pottery with this black paper label intact.

Pennsbury Pottery Marks

A 5" unmarked Plaque, probably Lewis Brothers, "Roll Out the Barrell". From the collection of Joyce Smalley.

A 5" Mug. Reverse side of "Jim" mug. Inferior quality piece marked Pennsbury, but probably Lewis Bros. From the collection of Joyce Smalley.

Obverse side of the same mug.

Collectors should be alerted to the fact there are look-a-likes in the Pennsbury field. Some are even marked "Pennsbury Pottery." When Pennsbury closed, in 1970, two employees from the Pottery gained employment at the Lewis Brothers Pottery in Trenton, New Jersey. These two girls were hired to assist their new employers on the technique of art type ware, since Lewis Brothers were not previously engaged in this type of production. During this same period, Lewis Brothers purchased fifty different molds from Pennsbury. According to the purchase contract, the name Pennsbury was to be removed. However, some pieces escaped this removal and were produced with the Pennsbury name exposed. No doubt, this was an honest mistake. On some pieces, where the name was not removed, the name Lewis Brothers was added to the marking.

The articles made, by Lewis Brothers, were a few pieces of table-wares (bowls, pitchers etc.), mugs, coasters and ash trays. The patterns were mostly the Amish, Hex and some Barber Shop Quartet. Some designs and sayings were changed, somewhat, to show variation. Some of the molds, purchased from Pennsbury, were duplicates. Also, some of these molds were changed slightly (e.g. hen and rooster sets). How many of these purchased molds were used is unknown since articles produced were made on order only. No Harvest or Rooster patterns (dinnerware line etc.), plaques, birds or any unusual molds; such as the highly decorated pieces were included in the purchase. After close examination of these look-a-like pieces, collectors will notice that the majority of these articles are heavier, in weight, and even some are somewhat lighter, in weight, than the authentic Pennsbury product. Every piece was not uniform.

Lewis Brothers did produce articles, in forms never used at Pennsbury, using a similar brown finish. These pieces were never marked at all. The Lewis Brothers products, that still bare the Pennsbury mark, were from badly worn molds and were very indistinct. These pieces are easily detected by a thin, dull, smeary glaze, some having a bisque-like appearance. These pieces were fired only once, while Pennsbury fired their products twice. In conclusion, all articles that are signed by hand are authentic Pennsbury.

Unmarked snack buckets, reputed to be Lewis Brothers (obverse side).

Reverse side of the same buckets.

Obverse side of a personalized Mug, made by Lewis Brothers. From the collection of Joyce Smalley.

Reverse side of the same Mug.

A 1970 Glen View Tree Tops Plate.

Glen View and Pennington Potteries

Shortly before the Pennsbury Pottery declared bankruptcy, in October, 1970, Mr. Sidney Sachs, who had been a jobber for Pennsbury products, opened his own business known as the Stumar Company, located at 5 South Eastern Road, Glenside, Pennsylvania. The operation soon became Glen View Pottery. According to the Pennsylvania Directory of Industries, in 1972 the Glen View Pottery was operating at 2650 W. Maple, Langhorne, Pennsylvania. The record shows two employees and Sidney Sachs as a partner in the business. Who the partner was is unknown. However, there have been rumors as to the possibilities.

At Glen View Pottery, Mr. Sachs continued to market the ever popular Stumar Christmas plates. An invoice has been discovered, dated September 8, 1970, showing a sale of one dozen 1970 Stumar Christmas plates. In 1971, Mr. Sachs introduced the Stumar Mother's Day plates. He also introduced a line of Pennsylvania Dutch, Amish type plates, all marked Glen View. Incidently, the Christmas plates and Mother's Day plates were in production through 1978. The 1970 Pennsbury Stumar "Angel" plate continued to sell considerably well as it was a very popular item and was distributed by both Glen View and Pennington with the original markings. This accounts for so many appearing on the secondary market today. All of these plates have the identical finish as the Pennsbury brown ware. Since Pennsbury closed in 1970, the Glen View Pottery continued to create the Tree Tops Christmas plates, with their own company mark, for Mr. and Mrs. Douglas K. Porteous, of Paoli, Pennsylvania. The first ten Tree Tops Christmas plates were produced by the Pennsbury Pottery (1960-1969). The final four (1970-1973) were made by Glen View, resulting in a total of fourteen in all. The company also continued to produce a line of mugs for the Bucks County Bar Association. Many other articles were commissioned and made for other companies and various organizations.

A 1971 Glen View Tree Tops Plate.

In 1975, Glen View sold out to Lenape Products, the parent company for the Pennington Pottery. An interview was arranged with two executives of Pennington and Lenape Products. Mrs. Helen F. Brown is president of the Pennington Pottery and an artist of considerable talent. Mr. Bill Owens is vice-

A 1972 Glen View Tree Tops Plate.

A 1973 Glen View Tree Tops Plate.

president and a former chemist. Mr. Peter K. Hexter is president of Lenape Products and marketing director of Pennington Pottery, Inc., Pennington, New Jersey. The question was asked, if Pennington continues to produce any articles that resemble anything Pennsbury produced. Mr. Peter Hexter stated, "The hand finished Mother's Day, Christmas, Pennsylvania Dutch line plates, and all hand decorated plates were definitely discontinued, in 1978, because the price received was too low for the amount of work necessary to create them. Apparently, the public seemed to prefer the porcelain plates instead."

The Lenape Products Company produces a line of bathroom china, drawer pulls, switch plates, and other novelties that are commissioned by various companies. Banks, made in the form of Hershey kisses, were made for the Hershey Chocolate Company, but this practice may have been discontinued.

The Stumar plates are approximately eight and one-half inches in diameter, just slightly larger than the 1970 Pennsbury "Angle" plate. The Mother's Day plates are extremely lovely, depicting adorable children and mothers. Each plate includes spring flowers worked around the center scene. One exception is the 1975, which is adorned with ivy leaves. Each colorful Christmas plate is decorated with holly, in addition to the center scene. The one exception is the 1976. The center scene on these plates depict seasonal activities, both indoors and outdoors.

All Glen View plates were designed by the talented artist and designer, Mary Jane Hillegass, and each plate is marked with her initials; mjh original. The Pennington plates, dated 1976 and 1977, were designed as a group effort. The final Mother's Day plate and Christmas plate, dated 1978 were·designed and signed by Maryanne Braun, a gifted artist, who is a niece of Mrs. Helen Brown. The Stumar line, in 1970, was created by Pennsbury, 1971 through 1975 by Glen View, and 1976 through 1978 by Pennington. The Pennington Company also produced pleasing "Collector Bells", duplicating the identical scenes that appear on the plate of the same date. The bells are not marked, but they are dated and initialed by the artist. These Christmas bells were produced for three years, 1976, 1977 and 1978. Mother's Day bells were only made in 1977 and 1978. Each of the bells is approximately 5½" tall and 3" wide, and each is equipped with a clapper.

The following list shows the titles and dates of each Stumar Christmas plate and Mother's Day plate.

Stumar Christmas plates:

1970—The Angel—First Edition

1971—The Old Canal

1972—Country Side

1973—Friendship

1974—Making Fancy

1975—Preparation

1976—Drummer Boy

1977—Joyful Expectations

1978—Christmas Is Giving

Stumar Mother's Day Plates:

1971—Mother In Flower Garden—First Edition

1972—Mother With Child

1973—Mother Quilting

1974—Mother At Cradle

1975—Mother Baking

1976—Mother Reading To Children

1977—Mother Comforting Child

1978—Tranquility—Molded in bas-relief

An 8½'' 1971 Mother's Day Plate, ''Mother in flower Garden''. A first editon, Stumar Plate, marked Glen View.

A 1972 Mother's Day Plate, "Mother with Child". Marked Glen View.

A 1974 Mother's Day Plate, "Mother at Cradle". Marked glen View.

A 1973 Mother's Day Plate, "Mother Quilting". Marked Glen View.

A 1975 Mother's Day Plate, "Mother Baking". Marked Glen View.

A 1976 Pennington Mother's Day Plate, "Mother Reading to Children." From the collection of Joyce Smalley.

A 1978 Mother's Day Plate, "Tranquility", Marked Pennington. final edition bas-relief. Signed M. Braun. From the collection of Joyce Smalley.

A 1977 Marked Pennington Mother's Day Plate, "Mother Comforting Child". From the collection of Joyce Smalley.

A 1977 Mother's Day Bell, "Mother's Comforting Child". signed GT.

1978 Mother's Day Bell (tranquility), 5½''. Signed M. Braum.

A 1977 Pennington Christmas Bell.

A 1976 Pennington Xmas Bell, ''Drummer Boy''. Signed AD.

A 1978 Pennington Christmas Bell, Children Feeding Squirrels, ''Christmas is Giving''. Signed Maryanne Braun.

A 1971 Christmas Plate, "The Old Canal". Marked Glen View.

A 1973 Christmas Plate, "Friendship". Marked Glen View.

A 1972 Christmas Plate, "Countryside". Marked Glen View.

A 1974 Christmas Plate, "Making Fancy". Marked Glen View.

A 1975 Christmas Plate, "Preparation". Marked Glen View.

A 1977 Christmas Plate, "Joyful Expectations". Marked Pennington.

A 1976 Christmas Plate, "Drummer Boy". Marked Pennington.

A 1978 Christmas Plate, "Christmas is Giving. Final edition, in bas-relief. Signed M. Braun.

A series of six charming Pennsylvania Dutch plates were made by both Glen View and Pennington Potteries. Each plate is eight and one-half inches in diameter, and each has the same border of incised tulips and leaves. In the six inch center, the scenes are all different, depicting Amish type people going about their daily routines. These extraordinary plates also have the identical brown finish as the Pennsbury Pottery with the figures painted in the appropriate colors. Each plate has an incised hand written title on the reverse side. These titles are:

#801 Courting Buggy

#802 At the Water Pump

#803 Barn Raising

#804 Feeding Geese

#805 School Days

#806 The Family

Each plate shows Amish type people in action, and all pieces have the appropriate company mark. Incidently, the accompaning numbers were obtained from a Glen View—Pennington catalog.

Two very interesting plates were introduced, by Pennington, as the "Egyptian" line. These are: "Ancient Egyptian Trilogy," dated 1977 and "Charioteer," dated 1978. This line was originally planned to include a series of six, limited to 5000, sequentially numbered. However, since production ceased in 1978, on all hand painted plates, the final four were never produced. The two original plates were sculptured, in bas-relief, by Sayed Khalifa, a native of Egypt. The plates are also hand painted. The color and decorations were designed by Mrs. Helen F. Brown. Before coming to the United States, Mr. Khalifa enrolled in the College of Science in Cairo, and later received the Gold Medal of Distinction in Sculpture for Egypt and Syria. He was highly recognized, by his native Country, for his talent in the art field. In 1968, Mr. Khalifa arrived in the United States and, in a very short time, he became a leader in the field of ceramic design and was commissioned by several prestigious companies in this country.

Glen View Pennsylvania Dutch line, "The Family".

Glen View, Pennsylvania Dutch "Courting Buggy". From the collection of Joyce Smalley.

Glen View, Pennsylvania Dutch "At the Water Pump". From the collection of Joyce Smalley.

An 8½'' Pennsylvania Dutch Glen View Plate, ''Barn Raising''. from the collection of Esther Keller. Signed GT. #803.

An 8½'' Pennsylvania Dutch Pennington Plate, ''School Days''. Signed G.T. #805.

The ''Trilogy'' plate depicts the heads of three dancers, of ancient Egypt, molded in bas-relief, hand painted in strict accordance with the fashion of that era. The ''Charioteer'' plate depicts a horse drawn chariot, with the driver clothed and decorated in colors that also reflect the mode of the period. The first Trilogy plate produced was presented, as a gift, to President Anwar Sadat of Egypt. Since Mr. Sadat was not in the United States, at that time, the plate was presented, by Mrs. Helen Brown and Mr. Peter Hexter, to the Egyptian Ambassador, Ashiaf Ghorbal, to be given to the Egyptian President at a later date. The presentation took place in Washington, D.C. at the Egyptian Embassey, on January 30, 1978, at 4:30 P.M.

These two very unusual plates, Trilogy and Charioteer, were produced from the finest faience and are ten and three-fourths inches in diameter. The designs are not American, but are authentic Egyptian type art.

Two plates called ''Seashore'' were produced applying the identical finish that was used on the Pennsylvania Dutch line. These plates depict the same scene of the ''Barnegat Lighthouse'' off the New Jersey shore line. The difference between these two plates is that Number 900 has the name inscribed on the reverse, while the number 901 is inscribed ''Barnegat Light'' on the obverse at the top of the plate. Number 901 is also lighter in color.

A line of six personalized plates, decorated with decals, using the same border as the one used on the Pennsylvania Dutch plates were created for births, and finished in a choice of brown or white. The titles of these plates are, Little Bo Peep, Little Miss Muffet, Little Boy Blue, Humpty Dumpty, Mary Mary and Baa Baa Black Sheep.

Other items produced, were plates and matching bell to be personalized for either weddings or wedding anniversaries. These picture a wedding bell on both plate and the bell. Both are finished in brown or white. These pieces were not hand decorated, but only decals were applied.

Among Pennington's commissioned articles were items made for the American Heritage Collection, including a reproduction of a Ming Cat doorstop, with authentic crackle glaze, which sold new for $87.50. Also created were cat statues in solid black, white or green. Three sizes

Ancient Egyptian Collector Series Plates
By Pennington Pottery

1977 "Trilogy" 10¾"

1978 "Charioteer" 10¾"

Production was limited to 5000 each, sequentially numbered.

"Trilogy" ——— The three dancers of Egypt. The plate is authentic in every detail, even to the caps of the dancers. It was a custom, at that time, to apply scented oils to the caps as the rapid tempo, of their dance, caused a rise in body temperature. The scented oils would flow, from the caps, to the rest of the costume, emitting an exotic fragrance as it flowed.

were made, small, medium and large. The large cat statue measures approximately fifteen inches tall.

Many small bric-a-brac pieces were manufactured in volume; such as a liberty bell showing the authentic crack. This piece is brown, trimmed in green and yellow bands inscribed "Spirit of America." The bell is not marked and does not come equipped with a clapper.

Mrs. Helen F. Brown, president of Pennington Pottery, states: "At this period in time, all products marked Pennington have been discontinued."

Glen View and Pennington Pottery Marks

Glen View and Pennington pottery is marked by the respective company that created the design. Some pieces are marked in script, by hand, while others are marked with a stamp, including a bird in the design. Each company used the same type of mark, with the exception of the Pottery name. It should be noted, here, that Glen View and Pennington continued distribution of their plates until 1978, using the original mark of the Pottery that first produced the pieces. This also includes the Pennsbury 1970 Christmas plate.

Names of artists whose monogram appears on some articles are:

Anna Marie Coxgrove AMC

Glenna Thorpe GT

Violet Kanivrael VK

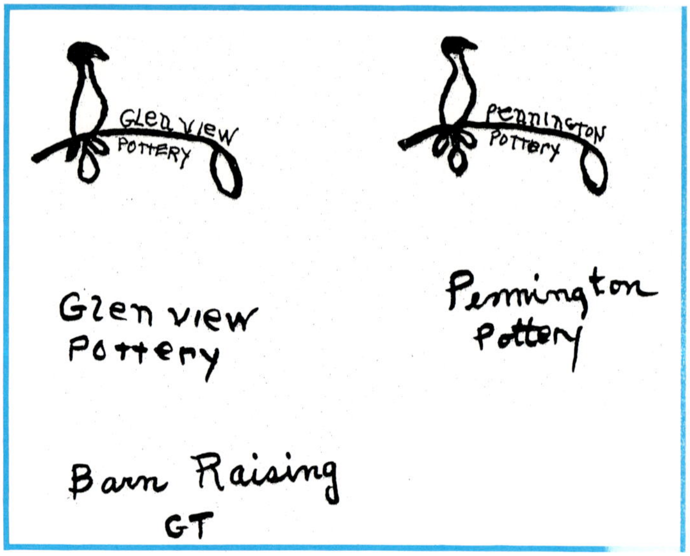

Red Rooster—20R

Black Rooster—20B

Pennsbury Pottery

PENNSBURY POTTERY, a low-slung, many-windowed building, is located just off Route 1, three miles west of Morrisville, in historic Bucks County, Pennsylvania. The business was founded in 1950 and brought through its infancy under the able guidance and supervision of Henry Below, a happy man with a great gift for making pottery. It was with Henry's talent in ceramics and good business sense, coupled with his wife's creative designs, that Pennsbury Pottery grew in so short a time to be known and liked across the continent.

Here in this catalog, you can see many of the fine pieces produced daily at Pennsbury Pottery. The beauty of hand-crafted pottery is ever present in the carved designs filled in with soft warm colors. Pennsbury Pottery ware, which is known for the authenticity of its Early Pennsylvania American motif, has captured a warm, folk hospitality which lends great charm to its use in table settings or as decorative pieces. The surrounding countryside is, of course, a reliable source for this authentic spirit and the quaint designs. Even the verses carry a gentle folk humor.

Should you be in Bucks County or nearby, you are cordially invited to be our guest. The doors of Pennsbury Pottery are always open. You will enjoy browsing through our showroom, and we make very good hosts.

ASH TRAYS — 8" SCALLOPED

1217-92
Hex

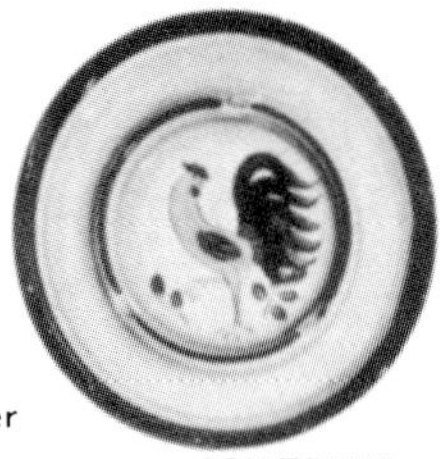

1053-20R
Red Rooster

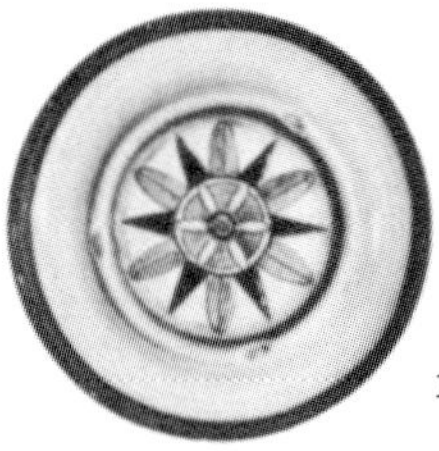

1053-92
Hex

1217-33
Amish

ASH TRAYS — 5" Round

1217-20R
Red Rooster

1217-20B
Black Rooster

1217-23
Don't be so Doppish

1217-25
What Ouches you

1217-26
Such Schmootzers

1217-27
Outen the Light

1217-31
Its Maken Down

ASH TRAYS — OCTAGONAL

1010-45
Two Birds over Heart

1010-52
Tulip in Heart

1010-67
Pink Tulip

1010-69
Crested Birds

1010-98
Horses

1010-287
Three Tulips

ASH TRAYS — RAILROAD

2103-4
"Star"
Central R.R. of N. J.

2103-5
"Tiger"
Pennsylvania R.R.

2103-6
"General"
Western & Atlantic R.R.

2103-7
"999"
New York Central & HRR

2103-8
"John Bull"
Camden & Amboy R.R.

2103-9
"C. D. Huntington"
Central Pac. R.R.

2103-10
"Lafayette"
Balt. & Ohio R.R.

2103-11
"Camelback"
Reading R.R.

2103-12
"Stourbridge Lion"
D. & H. R.R.

ASH TRAYS — SHIPS

2103-274 — Dreadnaught

2103-275 — Barkentine

2115-281 — Flying Cloud

2113-281
Flying Cloud

2103-284 — Schooner

2113-276 — Lightning

2113-277 — Raleigh

2114-279 — Constitution

2115-280 — Steam Boat

2114-278 — Charles W. Morgan

1192-20R
Red Rooster

1192-20B
Black Rooster

1310-91 — Dutch Talk

BOWLS — 11″ ROUND

1192-33
Amish

1192-91
Dutch Talk

BOWLS — 9″ ROUND

1030-37 — Boy & Girl

CAKE STANDS

1030-40 — Harvest

1030-45 — Two Birds over Heart

1030-74 — Family

BREAD PLATES

1279-57 — Oval Sheafs of Wheat

1280-57 — Round Sheafs of Wheat

1192-92
Hex

1192-303
Folkart

CANDY DISH — HEART

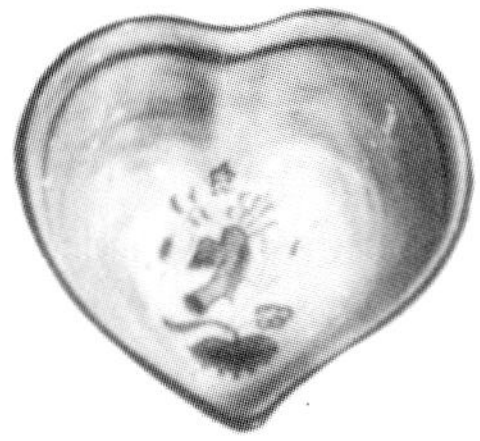

1235-68 — Bird over Heart

BUTTER DISH

1234-68 — Bird over Heart

COOKIE JARS

1226-20R
Red Rooster

1226-20B
Black Rooster

1226-40
Harvest

1226-75
Red Barn

1226-92
Hex

CRUET SETS

1236-81
Amish — Vinegar

1236-82
Amish — Oil

1236-20R
Red Rooster — Oil

1236-20R
Red Rooster — Vinegar

1236-20B
Black Rooster — Oil

1236-20B
Black Rooster — Vinegar

1077-61 — Barber Shop Quartet

1120-61 — 2 qt. pitcher
Barber Shop Quartet

BEER MUGS

1075-33
Amish

1075-50
Swallow the Insult

1075-56
Gay Ninety

1075-61
Barber Shop Quartet

1075-66
Fisherman

1075-286
Eagle

BEVERAGE MUGS

1218-20R
Red Rooster

1218-20B
Black Rooster

1218-75
Red Barn

1218-92
Hex

1218-303
Folkart

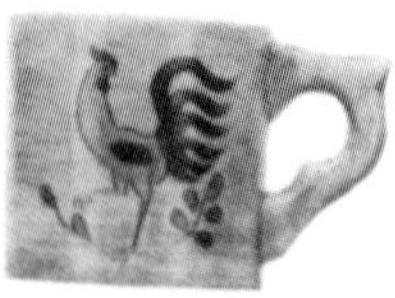
1167-20R
Red Rooster

1167-20B
Black Rooster

1167-286
Eagle

1167-303
Folkart

1167-75
Red Barn

1167-92
Hex

COFFEE MUGS

1167-62
"Luigi" — Barber Shop

1167-63
"Schultz" — Barber Shop

1167-64
"Olson" — Barber Shop

1167-65
"Horowitz" — Barber Shop

1167-33
Amish

1077-33 — Amish

1077-56 — Gay Ninety

1167-56
Gay Ninety

PRETZEL BOWLS

REVERE BOWLS

1077-286 — Pretzel bowl

1320 — 9″

1319 — 7″

1318 — 5″

EAGLEWARE

1119-286 — 1 qt. pitcher

1075-286 — Beer mug

1068-286 — 8″ plate

1167-286 — Coffee mug

1120-286 — 2 qt. pitcher

1004-EM — Cigarette box

2103-286 — Ash tray

1308-EM — Penholder

1300-EM — Ash tray — 3 rest

1288-EMF
6″ Sq. tile-framed

RED BARN WARE

1218-75
Beverage mug

1068-75 — 8″ plate

1119-75 — 1 qt. pitcher

1077-75 — Pretzel bowl

1167-75 — Coffee mug

DESK BASKETS

2013-20R
Red Rooster

2013-55
Two Women under Tree

2013-45
Two Birds over Heart

2013-68
Bird over Heart

2013-10
"Lafayette" B&O R.R.

2013-286
Eagle

WEDDING PLATES

1042-20R — Red Rooster

1029-37A — Boy and Girl

1029-45A — Two Birds over Heart

1042-20B — Black Rooster

1042-34 — Mother Serving Pie

1042-37 — Boy & Girl

1042-38 — Walking to Homestead

1042-92 — Hex

1042-39 — Picking Apples ·

1042-40 — Harvest

1042-41 — Making Pie

PITCHERS

Size Line-up — Miniature (2½" High)
Half Pint (3¾" High)
Pint (5" High)
1-Qt. (6¼" High)
2-Qt. (7¼" High)
3-Qt. (9¾" High)

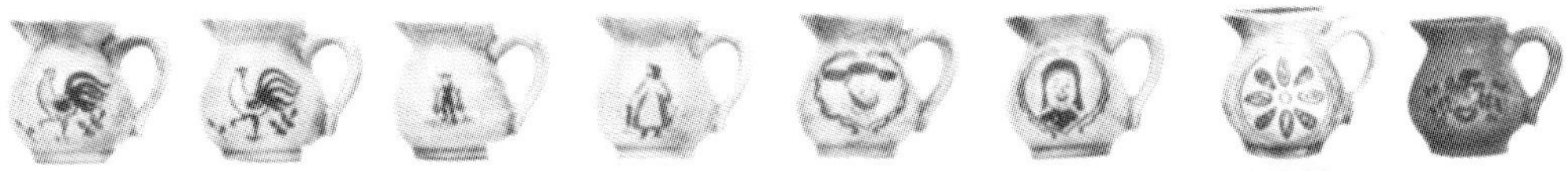

MINIATURE PITCHERS

1115-20R Red Rooster | 1115-20B Black Rooster | 1115-59 Amish Boy | 1115-60 Amish Girl | 1115-77 Amish Man | 1115-78 Amish Woman | 1115-92 Hex | 1115-303 Folkart

HALF PINT PITCHERS

1116-20R Red Rooster | 1116-20B Black Rooster | 1116-67 Tulip | 1116-77 Amish Man | 1116-78 Amish Woman | 1116-92 Hex | 1116-303 Folkart

PINT PITCHERS

1118-20R Red Rooster | 1118-20B Black Rooster | 1118-77 Amish Man | 1118-78 Amish Woman | 1118-92 Hex | 1118-303 Folkart

1119-20R Red Rooster | 1119-20B Black Rooster | 1119-33 Amish | 1119-75 Red Barn | 1119-92 Hex | 1119-286 Eagle | 1119-303 Folkart

1-QT. PITCHERS

1120-20R Red Rooster | 1120-20B Black Rooster | 1120-33 Amish | 1120-67 Tulip | 1120-92 Hex | 1120-286 Eagle

2-QT. PITCHERS

3-QT. PITCHERS

1121-20R Red Rooster | 1121-20B Black Rooster | 1121-67 Tulip

FISH

1054 — Round Fish

1099 — Large Fish

1102 — Small Long Fish

8" PLATES

1068-33 — Amish

1068-39 — Picking Apples

1068-40 — Harvest

1068-58 — Chatting

1068-72 — Courting Buggy

1068-73 — Family Wagon

1068-75 —- Red Barn

11" PLATES

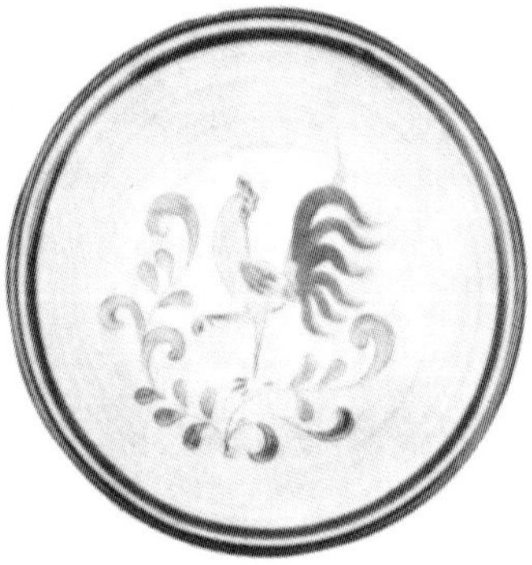

1029-20R — Red Rooster

1029-20B — Black Rooster

1029-40 — Harvest

1029-45 — Two Birds over Heart

1029-74 — Family

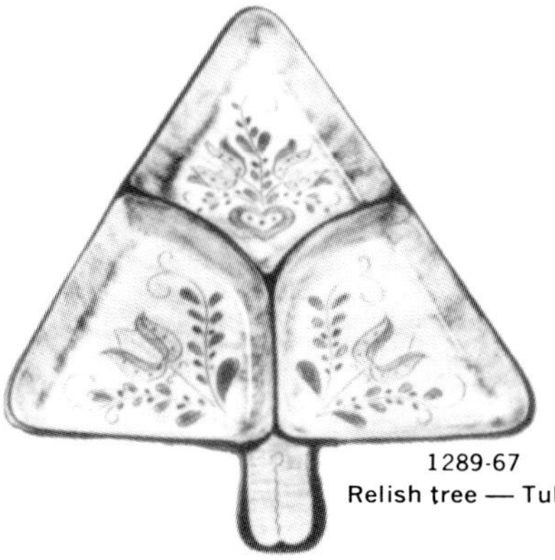

1289-67
Relish tree — Tulip

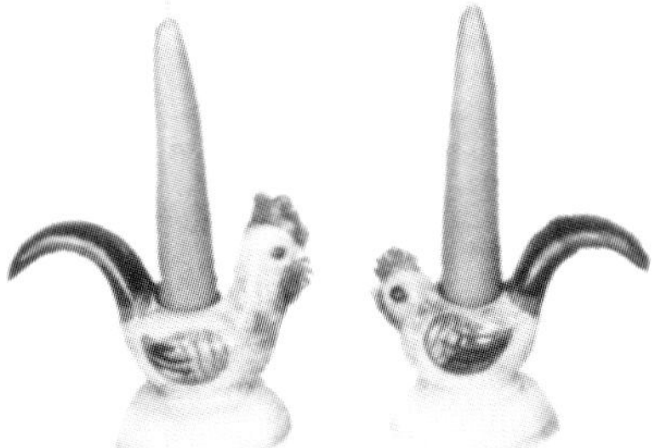

131-20RorB — Hen and Rooster

1112-20R
Red Rooster

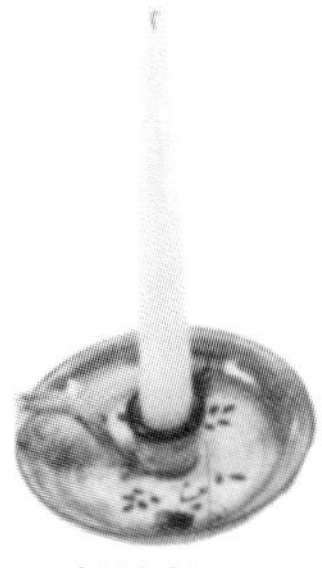

1112-20B
Black Rooster

CANDLE STICKS

1055-20R — Red Rooster

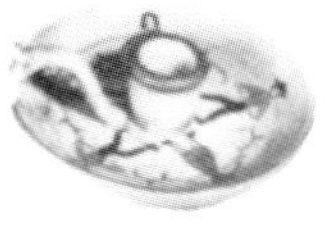

1112-33
Amish

1112-67
Tulip

1112-92
Hex

1055-20B — Black Rooster

6" TILES

1055-34
Mother Serving Pie

1055-35
Kissing over Cow

1055-36
Horse and Carriage.

1055-37
Boy & Girl

1055-38
Walking to Homestead

1055-39
Picking Apples

1055-40
Harvest

1055-41
Making Pie

1055-42
Picking Flowers

1055-43
Basket of Flowers

1055-46
Farm Scene

1237-8
Amish Heads Salt & Pepper

TILES — FRAMED — 6" SQ.
1288-20R — Red Rooster
1288-20B — Black Rooster
1288-92 — Hex
1055-M — 3-tiles mounted

1076-33S — Amish Sugar and Creamer

4" ROUND TILES

1186-20R
Red Rooster

1186-20B
Black Rooster

1186-23
Don't be so Doppich

1186-25
What Ouches You

1186-26
Such Schmootzers

1187-27
Outen the Light

1186-28
Pop's Halt Et

1186-29
When the Cock Crows

1186-30
Come the Back Way

1186-31
Making Down

1186-32
Whole Empty

1186-33
Amish

1153
4-cup teapot

1169
Cereal bowl

1193
Deep soup bowl

1234
Butter dish

DINNERWARE

1112
Candle stick

1030
Cake stand

1145
2-cup coffee pot

1226
Cookie jar

1218
Beverage mug

1027
5″ compote

1167
Coffee mug

1114
Salt and pepper

1165S
Snack set — cup & saucer

1222S
Small sugar and creamer set

All dinnerware shapes are available in 20R Red Rooster, 20B Black Rooster, 92 Hexware, 303 Folkart, as per price list.

1315 — 5″ Cyl. casserole w/cover

1316 — 7″ Cyl. casserole w/cover

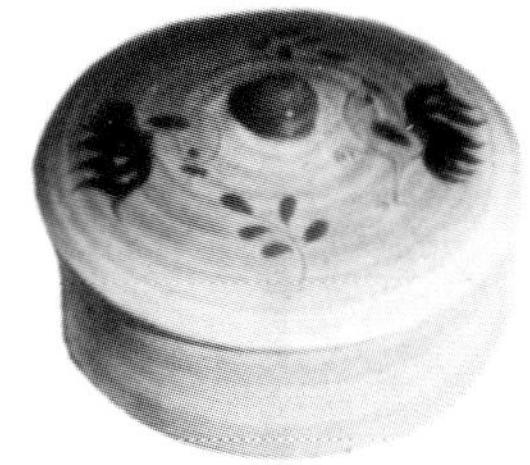

1317 — 9″ Cyl. casserole w/cover

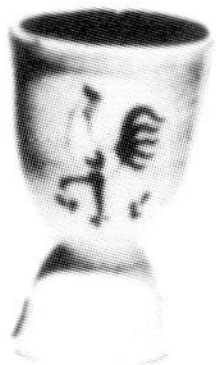

1224
Egg cup

2013
Desk basket

1219
Small casserole w/cover

1163 — Tureen w/cover and ladle

1164S
Cup and saucer

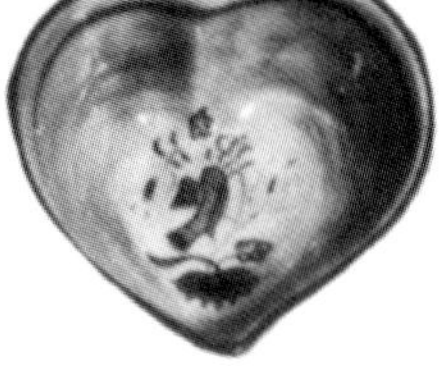

1235
Heart candy dish

1200
8″ x 11″ Oval platter

1277
11″ x 14″ Oval platter

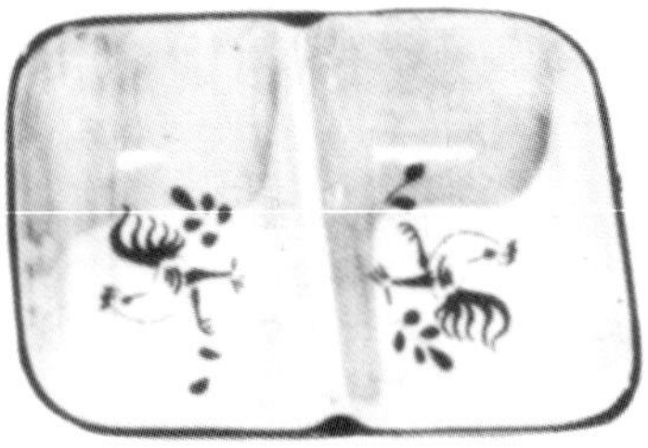

1049
Divided vegetable bowl

1241
13″ Round salad bowl

1296 — Gravy boat

1031 — Cheese & cracker dip

1076S — Sugar and creamer set

1173
6-cup coffee pot

1292
Canister — tea

1295
Canister — sugar

1294
Canister — flour

1293
Canister — coffee

Folkart — 303

Hexware — 92

Index—General

Index—Line Names and Patterns